SIX TIRES, NO PLAN

SIX TIRES, NO PLAN

THE IMPOSSIBLE JOURNEY
OF THE MOST INSPIRATIONAL LEADER
THAT (ALMOST) NOBODY KNOWS

MICHAEL ROSENBAUM

GREENLEAF
BOOK GROUP PRESS

Published by Greenleaf Book Group Press
Austin, Texas
www.gbgpress.com

Distributed by Greenleaf Book Group LLC

For ordering information or special discounts for bulk purchases, please
contact Greenleaf Book Group LLC at PO Box 91869, Austin, TX 78709,
512.891.6100.

Design and composition by Greenleaf Book Group LLC and Bumpy Design
Cover design by Greenleaf Book Group LLC

Publisher's Cataloging-In-Publication Data
(Prepared by The Donohue Group, Inc.)
Rosenbaum, Michael A.
  Six tires, no plan : the impossible journey of the most inspirational leader that
(almost) nobody knows / Michael Rosenbaum. — 1st ed.
   p. ; cm.
  ISBN: 978-1-60832-257-2
  1. Halle, Bruce T. 2. Discount Tire Company. 3. Tire industry—United
States. 4. Businessmen—United States—Biography. 5. Dealers (Retail trade)—
United States. I. Title.
HD9161.5.T574 R67 2012
381/.45/6292482/092   2011933414

Part of the Tree Neutral® program, which offsets the number of trees
consumed in the production and printing of this book by taking proactive
steps, such as planting trees in direct proportion to the number of trees used:
www.treeneutral.com

TreeNeutral

Printed in the United States of America on acid-free paper

15 16 17 18 19   11 10 9 8 7 6 5 4 3

First Edition

ACKNOWLEDGMENTS

This story was already written when I arrived for my first meeting at Discount Tire Company. It was drafted by Bruce Halle and thousands of people who have signed on to fulfill both his life mission and their own. Truly, I am just the guy who typed it up.

I was introduced to the Bruce Halle story by Marilyn Seymann, Ph.D., who is CEO of the Bruce T. Halle Family Foundation and the kind of friend one should hope to find once in a lifetime. When Marilyn suggested this project, I was hesitant. After publication of my fourth book, I was taking some time off from writing. A biography of a tire retailer didn't seem to be the project that would lure me back to writing books.

"Wait until you meet Bruce. You'll feel differently," Marilyn said. As always, she was right.

I am grateful to Marilyn for that introduction and for the access that both Bruce and his wife, Diane, offered in the development of this project. Their willingness to discuss situations candidly and address challenges honestly has improved the reporting in this text.

Similarly, I am most appreciative of the openness provided by dozens of employees who agreed to speak candidly and, usually, on the record about their boss. It's always a tightrope act to speak publicly about the guy who signs your paycheck, which makes the staff contribution to my research even more valuable.

Special thanks must go to Marlene Ambrose, Bruce Halle's executive assistant, whose consistent cooperation and coordination efforts made this project much more productive, and to Carol Woyak, administrative assistant to Diane Halle, for her invaluable support.

Thanks, as well, to Gary Van Brunt, vice chairman; Tom Englert, chief executive officer; and Steve Fournier, chief operating officer, for repeated reviews of history and operating philosophy. Lori Governale, vice president of administration; Andrew Haus, assistant treasurer; and Stacy Adams, assistant vice president of human resources/payroll, all provided invaluable support in helping me sort out dates and facts about the company. Mike Schwerd, senior advertising analyst, was irreplaceable as a guide to the company's photo archives.

Thanks to Odette Leclerc, curator at the Berlin and Coos County Historical Society, for research into the early life of Bruce Halle and his family in Berlin, New Hampshire.

Thanks to Marcee Williams and my wife, Jill, for countless hours of transcription and proofreading, along with the team at Greenleaf Book Group for shepherding this project to completion.

Finally, a great thank-you to the guys in the stores, both full-time and part-time, who shared their stories and dreams with me. You have inspired me and I wish you the greatest of success. After meeting so many of you, I know you will achieve it.

—MICHAEL ROSENBAUM

CONTENTS

FOREWORD

In 1960, two years before Sam Walton opened his first Walmart store in Rogers, Arkansas, Bruce Halle rented an empty shop in Ann Arbor, Michigan, and founded Discount Tire Company. Half a century later, both companies are industry leaders with strong cultural drivers. While Halle's story is less studied than Walton's, the growth of Discount Tire offers significant insights into the creation of a sustainable, productive business.

Both founders began with a commitment to lower prices than those offered by other retailers. Both went further, however, by focusing on the customer's experience as a way to build repeat sales and referrals. Although both would sell products that consumers could buy elsewhere, each man found a way to differentiate his business, creating favorable relationships with customers and strong brand value.

Brand value, of course, is the whole that exceeds the sum of its parts. Brand value offers a competitive advantage that can be measured in customer loyalty, marketing effectiveness, cost of capital, or all of the above.

Given the importance of this advantage, business schools and students invest substantial energy in the study of brands. Often, the corporations studied are mature, with established strategies and mission statements. In many cases, it would serve these scholars well to start at the beginning, at the founding of the companies they study.

When an entrepreneur opens a business, the essence of its brand is established before the first sale. Entrepreneurs imbue their creations with passions and values that translate into corporate brands. Like Sam Walton and most other business founders, Bruce Halle did not bring a detailed business plan to the tire store he opened in 1960. He did, however, bring a set of values to drive his decisions.

At the most basic level, Halle wanted to put food on the table. His first goals were primal: food, clothing and shelter. Somewhat more sophisticated were the values he applied to achieve these goals. Halle was willing to accept a discounter's margins, but wanted to earn loyalty and referrals in return. He was willing to work hard, but wanted to have fun while doing it. He wanted to be in charge, but knew he couldn't become truly successful without the support of a team.

Notably, like Walton, Halle didn't begin with a spreadsheet of financial projections, but focused instead on the value to be delivered to the customer. For the entrepreneur, strategic plans and vision statements are seldom a priority. The founder's life is focused on the next customer, the next sale, the next bill to be paid, and the personal approach to life that translates into business practice.

As the entrepreneur establishes a business, the corporate brand is a personal brand, reflecting the specific relationships created by the founder with customers, suppliers and other stakeholders. The brand is idiosyncratic, tied to the individual entrepreneur's passions and values. In fact, the founder is the brand. If his or her values are constructive and the founder is consistent in delivering on them, the company will grow.

To accelerate and sustain that growth, the founder must propagate the personal brand across a larger base of customers. The founder must enlist likeminded employees—true believers—to both adopt and fulfill the mission. Employees must be convinced, not compelled, to sign on to the founder's vision and values, to operate in a way that resembles or replicates the founder's style. Employees must become missionaries for the personal brand of the founder.

In the broadest sense, the brand represents the overall reputation and identity of the company among all stakeholder groups. More important, the brand reflects specific relationships of individual employees and customers. Whether the employee is a Discount Tire store manager or a Walmart greeter, local representatives of the founder's values will drive sustainable success.

As a company grows, the founder's values may be codified into a mission statement that is transmitted and translated for newer members of the team. When the mission remains clear and the values are shared consistently, the company has the greatest opportunity to build and reinforce its brand.

Notably, values include attributes that are not tied immediately to product delivery. In the case of Discount Tire, Halle emphasizes the importance of paying forward, creating opportunity for the next employee. The type of person who will respond to Halle's passion is also likely to believe strongly in the team, the community, the company and its customers. As they mirror the founder's values and pay forward to stakeholders, they become missionaries for the brand and build the company.

Is it possible to overemphasize the connection between the values of the founder and the long-term sustainability of a corporation? Certainly, the linkage might become less obvious over time, but it would be a mistake to presume that the link can be broken without a negative impact. If the founder's values are both productive and consistently applied, they will drive growth. As employees adopt those values, the corporate culture evolves to accelerate and sustain growth over the long term.

This is demonstrably the case for Discount Tire. The culture of customer service, of paying forward, of supporting fellow employees, is clearly a continuation of Bruce Halle's value system. As a driver of sustained growth and financial strength, the value of this culture is indisputable.

Creating and maintaining a cohesive, productive business approach is a challenge for all companies. Few will succeed at this exercise for more than a handful of years. Even rarer, of course, are companies like Discount Tire, or Walmart, that can thrive after more than half a century.

When one encounters a large organization with a committed team of brand champions, it's instinctive to look for the sophisticated strategy behind the culture. It's often more instructive, however, to look to the company's founding, and its founder. In many cases, possibly most, the seeds were present at the beginning.

S. Robson Walton
Chairman of the Board
Wal-mart Stores, Inc.

INTRODUCTION

More than six miles above the Gulf Coast, Bruce Halle is saying grace.

It is a moment that will pass unnoticed by his colleagues at Discount Tire Company. Halle's lunch is laid out in front of him, his head is bowed and he is speaking softly. But he has not announced to the passengers on his jet that this is the time for everyone to say grace. Each person has his meal and each is free to do, or not do, as his individual practice directs.

It's a Bruce Halle moment. This is his jet, these are his employees and this is Halle's food that everyone is about to consume. For many corporate chieftains, this also would be the moment to insist that each employee follow the leader. Halle passes up the opportunity, following his own compass without demanding that others mimic his behavior.

Often, in the process of identifying the secrets to Halle's success, it's important to focus on the things that don't happen. Halle doesn't insist on being the center of every discussion, he doesn't discuss his possessions as if they were trophies on a wall, and you can talk to him for days on end without ever, ever having a conversation about tires.

Truth be told, Bruce Halle does not love tires. He doesn't love tire stores, either, even though he has amassed an empire of more than eight hundred retail tire stores over the five decades since his founding of Discount Tire Company.

What Halle does love is paying forward, creating the opportunity for the next guy who is willing to work hard to build a life and pay forward to the guy after that. He loves to see his own success reflected—and created—through the success of other people.

This is the story of an everyday hero, a very ordinary guy who overcame obstacles to lead a very extraordinary life. It's the story of an average Joe who makes it possible for thousands of other average Joes to become everyday heroes in their own right.

At first, people might question the idea that anything can be "everyday" about Bruce Halle and his life. The man is a billionaire, after all, the owner of a multibillion-dollar company and a legend in his industry. He goes where he wants when he wants, and when he arrives, the door is always open.

Money is the root of misperceptions, though, the Rorschach test of our own values. Many people will ascribe superior taste and judgment to the most basic acts of the wealthy. Others will dismiss any kindness as meaningless, arguing that *they can afford it.*

In that regard, money is also the great unequalizer, casting the actions and lives of the wealthy in a different hue than those of people with more limited resources. Remove the camouflage of wealth, though, and it is easier to see the man behind the means.

Bruce Halle was a poor kid and a poorer student, lacking focus, bedeviled by an unpredictable temper, often the loser in his battles of conscience, unsure of where or how he would find any direction in life.

In the ironic alchemy that creates everyday heroes, he was the perfect candidate.

Over the course of a lifetime, Halle has created a legacy not by building on innate gifts but by finding a way to get past his own limitations and find a new spark for good. He made as many mistakes as anyone else along the way, but he did two things that most people fail to do: he learned from his mistakes and he made it a practice to blame nobody but himself when things went awry.

That's the thing about everyday heroes. They aren't born to greatness or with superhuman powers. Trace the history of almost all of them and they will have seemed to have, more or less, the same capability and the same potential as any other person on the block. The people who make the leap are those who do more, who go beyond, who make the extra effort. Beyond the celebrity buzz, we admire people most when they walk the walk.

Bruce Halle walks the walk. His greatest achievement isn't tied to the wealth he's accumulated or the number of tires he's sold. What makes Halle special is his consistent, disciplined application of Golden Rule basics to create opportunity for thousands of ordinary guys who want to do more, go beyond and make the extra effort—even if they don't realize it at the time they join his company.

For many business leaders, success flows from the income statement, from market share and accumulation of personal wealth. For Halle, success is measured by the legions of tire changers who strive to model their careers, and their lives, after the guy who gave them their first real opportunity to succeed.

Since starting Discount Tire more than five decades ago, Halle has consistently paid forward to a new generation of ordinary Joes and motivated them to pay forward, as well. As they do so, they follow the path of the debt-ridden Marine who set the wheels in motion in an old plumbing supply store in Ann Arbor, more than fifty years ago.

This is the story of a very ordinary guy who has established a very extraordinary legacy.

THE BACK OF THE STORE

Bruce Halle is smiling as he climbs out of the minivan and surveys the Discount Tire store on Beach Boulevard. It's a beautiful spring day in Jacksonville, Florida, sunny and not too humid. In the bays, tire jockeys are working on a handful of cars. Out in the parking lot, the store's owner, James Turnage, is waiting to greet Halle and his team.

Technically, Turnage doesn't own the store. Every tire and wheel, the equipment and signage, the building itself and the land beneath all belong to Bruce T. Halle, founder and sole shareholder of Discount Tire Company. FLJ05—the fifth store opened in Jacksonville, Florida—is one of more than eight hundred stores in the retail empire Halle started in an old plumbing supply building in Ann Arbor, Michigan, more than fifty years ago.

In a very real sense, though, FLJ05 doesn't belong to Halle. Although he does own the physical property, Turnage owns the keys.

Discount Tire Company has no franchises and no equity investors other than Bruce Thomas Halle, but Halle wants Turnage and every other employee to think of the store as his own—and treat both employees and customers accordingly. While Turnage doesn't own title to the store, he does earn the same kind of returns any minority partner might. In addition to a base salary, he and Halle share in the earnings of the store: Turnage gets 10 percent of the first $200,000 in earnings and 20 percent of every dollar of earnings above that level. As would be the case with any other owner, there's no cap to his earnings potential. The model at Discount Tire is different from the many retailers that set a salary for store managers and then offer a potential bonus of, perhaps, 10 to 30 percent. Because 80 to 90 percent of store earnings flow back to the company, Halle sees no reason to limit the potential earnings of his managers.

This model has fulfilled a dream for thousands of blue-collar guys and they, in turn, have brought Discount Tire to the top spot among independent tire retailers. Discount Tire stores operate in twenty-three states from Florida to Washington, with many of its West Coast outlets operating as America's Tire stores. (The company opened store #800, an America's Tire shop in Rocklin, California, in May 2011.) The company expands its reach with its online Discount Tire Direct, which ships tires and wheels across the country. With stores in fewer than half of the states, Discount Tire captured an estimated 10 percent of the replacement tire market in 2011, posting more than $3 billion of revenues.

Along the way, Halle has joined the *Forbes* list of the world's richest people, and everyday guys like James Turnage have gained an opportunity they never envisioned when they entered the workforce.

The deal is simple. Halle personally scouts out the location for each store, and the company supplies the capital to buy or lease the property, build the store and provide the inventory and equipment. As store manager, Turnage is responsible for hiring, training, marketing, scheduling, customer service and cost control—the same responsibilities Halle had with his first store more than fifty years ago.

Halle has made a promise to his people: *do a good job and I'll provide lifelong opportunity for you.* Following that simple promise, Discount Tire has increased its revenues in every single year since 1960 and has never implemented a layoff.

Like most store managers—and like Halle himself—Turnage never thought about the tire business as a career when he was growing up. He had no specific career goals in mind, but he had a good personality, customer focus and a willingness to work hard. He was selling electronics at a Circuit City store in Tallahassee when one of the people he was waiting on, a Discount Tire store manager, suggested he come in for an interview.

Turnage showed up at the store as a truck arrived to deliver tires, so he ended up spending most of his interview time with the rest of the team, unloading the truck. "Really, this is my interview?" he asked—but he liked the people and the team environment. They liked him as well, and he took the job.

Turnage didn't start out as a store manager. Nobody starts with his own store at Discount Tire, even people who were managing a store somewhere else before joining the company. The company starts all its operating employees as part-time tire techs, the people who do most of the tire changing in the bays, or, rarely, as full-time assistant managers.

Since Halle started the company in 1960, this practice has been a sacred promise at Discount Tire. Nobody gets the keys to the store without starting out in a lower level, busting tires.

Just like Bruce T. Halle.

That consistent policy of promotion from within creates enormous loyalty among Halle's employees. At the corporate office, every operating executive up to CEO Tom Englert began his career where Turnage began, and where Halle began—in the back of a Discount Tire store.

Ostensibly, Halle is visiting FLJ05 to learn more about "roles-based management," which is essentially a codification of practices long in effect throughout the company. Each store manager has three or four assistant managers, and the roles-based approach defines each assistant's responsibilities more specifically. One assistant takes responsibility for work scheduling, another for marketing and another for the six-step sales process. From a management perspective, authority is more clearly defined through this approach. As a training tool, roles-based management makes each assistant more of an expert as he rotates through the core functions on the way to getting the keys to his own store.

The roles-based approach was developed by Ed Kaminski, vice president of Discount Tire's San Antonio region. Kaminski has delivered the highest level of sales per store among all twenty-three regions in the company, and Halle suggested that his other regional vice presidents take a look at what Kaminski was doing right. Greg Smith, vice president in Florida and Turnage's boss, took Kaminski's ideas, added a few refinements and became the leading teacher of the system.

"There's nothing wrong with stealing a good idea," Halle says, echoing an idea he himself had stolen from Sir Tom Farmer, his longtime friend and the founder of Kwik-Fit Holdings, the largest auto repair chain in Europe. Farmer sought reputation-management advice from Halle in the mid-1980s, and Halle, in turn, picked up a number of productive ideas from his Scottish colleague. While Halle encourages his people to steal good ideas, including this one, the corporate management team has issued no edicts to force adoption of Kaminski's program.

Ideas are more powerful and supported when they percolate from the ground up, instead of coming down as pronouncements from on high, says Florida VP Smith. Rather than announcing strategies du jour from the home office, Discount Tire relies on interaction among store managers within regions and connections among the regional officers to develop and transmit good ideas.

"All we did was take Ed Kaminski's idea and make it a little better," Turnage explains, referring to an executive he has never worked for in a region one thousand miles away. "Ed is always coming up with good ideas, so I always want to know what Ed is doing."

The roles-based system is remarkably simple. Turnage shows Halle a number of sheets that describe the corporate strategy and the responsibilities of each manager, then brings Halle back to the service bays to show him the system for implementation: three clipboards. Each assistant manager tracks his work on clipboards that anyone can see. Each employee can check progress or gaps at any time on any clipboard.

Rae Huckleberry, senior assistant manager and the guy in charge when Turnage is gone, runs through his role. It's his job to make sure each customer is taken care of properly, from the welcome to product delivery to the benediction—thanking the customer and asking for continued patronage and referrals. He also shows Halle the racks with this week's promotions and featured tires and wheels. The corporate office doesn't decide which products to promote at the store; that decision is left to the store managers as well.

Halle is familiar with the program, but he listens and responds as if he's hearing about it for the first time. He makes no suggestions about refinements or improvements. Halle knows quite a bit about running tire stores, but nothing about the specifics of FLJ05, and Turnage is doing just fine without Halle's help. Halle's job is not to micromanage but to support and inspire.

In fact, supporting and inspiring is the real reason for the site visit, and it turns out to be the best part of Halle's job. Five decades after starting the company and more than twenty years since the last time he rolled up his sleeves and helped unload a truck in one of his stores, Halle still thinks of himself as one of the guys. Spending time in the stores, chatting with the workers, he works to bridge the distance that would naturally develop between a nineteen-year-old kid busting tires and the owner of eight hundred tire stores.

In the corporate office, Halle often greets employees by asking, "What can I do for you today?" He will walk in on meetings to listen for a few minutes, make a minimal number of comments and express thanks to his employees for their contributions to the company. On days when his assistant, Marlene Ambrose, serves lunch in his office, Halle will return the favor by busing his table and putting his plates in the dishwasher. Halle builds morale like he built his company: from the bottom up. On the road, he is likely to spend more time with the service people in a store than he does with his managers.

At his first opportunity at FLJ05, Halle heads back to the bays, where tire techs are working on customers' cars. He walks from bay to bay, introducing himself to the techs he hasn't met on a previous visit and thanking them for their work. During some visits, a tire jockey will hesitate before extending a greasy hand to the founder, but Halle likes to remind them that his hands were just as grimy when he was in their shoes. Halle asks each tech about his family, how he got to Discount Tire and how he likes his job. The next time any of these employees meets Halle—and there probably will be a next time—he will be surprised at how much Halle remembers about this encounter.

Much of Halle's success flows from his retail focus—each store is uniquely important, each customer is uniquely valuable and each employee is a priceless individual. He never talks to the tire techs about tires, focusing instead on their lives and dreams, families and school. As the management team members traveling with Halle congregate in the parking lot, ready to move on to the next location, Halle is still in the back of the shop, chatting with the techs.

It's a pattern that repeats itself during the next store visit of that day. At FLJ06, a few miles away, Halle's first stop is the tire bays, where he spends ten minutes with the techs before focusing on the presentation by Emmanuel Perona, store manager. Gary Van Brunt, vice chairman, and James Silhasek, executive vice president and general counsel, chat with a few customers waiting for service while Michael Zuieback, executive vice president and chief strategy officer, talks with Perona. Halle, though, is drawn back to the bays, where he thanks the techs again and encourages a truck owner to bring more of his vehicles to Discount Tire.

As was the case at Turnage's store, the management team will wait in the parking lot while Halle finishes his good-byes with an extended thank-you to the tire techs. Halle has dined at the White House, won dozens of business honors and received the Order of St. Gregory—knighthood—from the Vatican, but the back of a tire store is still home.

At the end of every site visit, he never seems quite ready to leave that home. In a very real sense, he never will. This is where it all began.

A NORMAL CHILDHOOD

Fred Halle was one of the lucky ones, although it's difficult to imagine that he recognized his great fortune at the time.

In November of 1930, as the Great Depression spread across the globe, Fred could no longer support his wife and two boys in Springfield, Massachusetts. With limited prospects, Fred and Molly Halle were packing their scant possessions and preparing to return home to Berlin, New Hampshire, where they would live with Molly's parents. For the free-spirited Frederick Joseph Halle, twenty-seven years old and busted, the road ahead could not have looked promising.

Fred had been destined for the stage. Any stage. His French-Canadian grandfather, Alfred Antoine Halle, had come to Berlin from Quebec in the mid-1880s with his wife and two sons. In 1904, he bought the meat department from the C.C. Gerrish & Company grocery on Main Street, where he had worked as a butcher for nine years. With his eldest son, Wilfred, he established the Alfred Halle & Son meat market in the basement of the Gerrish Building. As they began their multigenerational enterprise, the Halles invented the Blanchette Sausage. The hot dog-sized concoction includes garlic, cloves, cinnamon and sage, and nostalgic residents can still order the "Halle Sausage" in a few restaurants in Berlin.

Just as Alfred's eldest son, Wilfred, had joined his father in the business, Wilfred's eldest, Frederick Joseph Halle, would naturally become the heir to the thriving shop. Fred wasn't made for business, however, and showed little interest in following in the family tradition.

A natural athlete and a talented singer and dancer, Fred sought out pretty much any vocation that would draw a crowd. He won a place on the track, basketball and football teams at Berlin High School, where he also sought the limelight as a member of the glee club. He competed in local Golden Gloves competitions in Berlin and tried out for a spot as a catcher with the Boston Braves farm team as well, but his true love was the stage.

After high school, Fred joined the Mayo Producing Company of Springfield, Massachusetts, as a traveling player. In Berlin, he played in Mayo's minstrel show to support a local boys' camp and took the lead role in the comedy *Some Boy*. By the time he married his high-school sweetheart, Mary Elizabeth (Molly) McKelvey, in 1927, he listed his occupation as a producer.

The Halle wedding at St. Kieran's Catholic Church represented a major detour in the life of Fred and Molly. Molly left her job of five years as a stenographer at Brown Company, the local paper mill, a month before the wedding. The newlyweds would leave immediately after the wedding for a new life 180 miles away, in Springfield, Massachusetts. Fred and Molly's first child, Fred Jr., would be born later that year.

The Halles scratched out a living in their new town, but the world changed for the worse as a recession that began in the summer of 1929 exploded into the Great Depression. When Wall Street cratered on Black Friday—October 29, 1929—Molly and Fred were anticipating the birth of their second child, Bruce, who joined them on May 27, 1930. Fred and Molly held out for a few more months in their adopted city, but finally made the decision to return home to Berlin.

Fred, Molly, Fred Jr. and Bruce moved into the home of Molly's parents, John and Catherine McKelvey, in the shadow of Mount Forist and a few blocks from St. Kieran's Catholic Church. Back in the town he and his wife had left three years earlier, unable to afford a place of his own, Fred Halle's wings had been clipped.

In light of the times, however, the Halle family was among the luckier residents of Berlin, New Hampshire, in the 1930s. Fred found work at the Berlin Fire Department, first as a firefighter and ultimately as deputy chief. Unlike many of his neighbors, Fred held a job throughout the Depression and, though the pay wasn't substantial, his new role as a fireman offered him opportunities to return to the spotlight.

Fred taught boxing to local boys, led a Boy Scout troop with Father Francis Curran, the priest at St. Kieran's and a longtime friend, and played Santa Claus at Christmas parties at the firehouse or VFW hall. He and Molly joined the choir at St. Kieran's, and Molly led a Girl Scout troop as she settled in to taking care of her children and, at times, her parents at 789 Third Avenue.

The Halles' new life was extraordinarily ordinary for the time. Fred worked while Molly managed the family's finances and cared for their rapidly growing family. The Halle's third son, Robert, had been born in 1932, James in 1935, Alan in 1936 and, later, daughters Mary Ellen in 1941 and Elizabeth (Betty) Louise in 1942. The local parish was a close-knit center of both religious and social activities for the devoutly Catholic couple. Their extended family of Halles and McKelveys comprised their safety net and the settings for holiday dinners.

Molly's half-brother, Charles, lived across the street from St. Kieran's with his wife, Kathleen, and their children. Nieces Louise and Charlotte McKelvey babysat Molly's younger children, and John Joseph McKelvey, Molly's nephew, became one of Bruce Halle's best friends. Fred and Molly's family visited after church at Charles and Kathleen's home and, on Halloween, the McKelveys would go trick-or-treating at the McKelvey/Halle home on Third Avenue.

The families camped out in the summers at Dolly Copp, about twenty miles from Berlin in the White Mountains. The men dug holes next to their tents, filling the holes with ice to refrigerate their food. They'd work in town during the day and return to the campgrounds at night to join their families.

"I think I had a normal childhood," Bruce Halle recalls today. "I can't remember anything being hard about it, just a normal family growing up. What does it mean? Normal? There were no real big problems with my life as a child growing up. I just moved along and got older each year. No bad things happened."

To Bruce Halle, growing up in a small town during the Depression was quite normal, at least in the sense that every child sees his unique experience as normal. Berlin had been staggered by the loss of jobs in the paper mill whose stench was the smell of prosperity to local residents. Bruce noticed the Civilian Conservation Corps trucks coming through town, fulfilling the economic stimulus of his day by finding government-funded work for unemployed men, but the depth and impact of unemployment were not topics for a youngster's mind.

"We were little Catholic kids and we were growing up in a small town. The church was a mile away, or whatever it was, and we went to church every Sunday with Mom and Dad," Halle remembers. "We had the nuns and they were teaching religion, along with other subjects. We weren't exposed to much else. All we had was radio, and the only thing I can remember listening to on the radio with my dad was fights—Joe Louis and Tony Galento and people like that fighting on radio. It was kind of cool. My dad was a fight kind of guy, so we always listened to fights."

It was the heyday of professional boxing in the United States. Jack Johnson ruled the heavyweight world in 1915, followed by such luminaries as Jess Willard, Jack Dempsey, Gene Tunney and Max Schmeling. Early in the century, professional boxing, like vaudeville, was a strictly local engagement to be seen in person. As radio began to proliferate in the 1920s, however, broadcasts of boxing matches became a major source of entertainment. By the time Bruce Halle was listening to Joe Louis and "Two Ton" Tony Galento in the late 1930s, boxing was a religion for many men and boys. Having a father who really could beat up any other kid's dad was a decidedly cool source of pride for the Halle boys, who saw their dad as larger than life.

Fred's talents did not extend to woodworking or other mechanical pursuits, so he relied on his friends at the firehouse to make skis and a

14

springboard—essentially a toboggan that can be steered—for his sons. Fred Jr., Bruce, Bob, Jim and Alan sledded down Third Avenue in the winter snow and had their names painted on the side of the big sled. Most exciting for the boys, their dad taught them how to box.

"We really looked up to him," recalls Bob Halle. "He was not just a physically strong man, but he was a good father, a loving father. He spent as much time as he could with his kids."

While dad was the hero, Molly managed the household quietly and within the meager budget provided by Fred's work. Bruce admired his father as a larger-than-life hero, but he revered his mother as a selfless worker and role model. "She was a lady. She was a manager. She was the brains of the family," he recalls today. "Dad was a great guy, but Mom handled the finances and that kind of thing. Mom was charming, sweet and nice, where Dad was the hit man, the muscle."

Molly was the first of many women and men who would appeal to Bruce as somewhat more socially skilled, smart and polished than his image of himself. As a boy in the 1930s, and as his father's son, Bruce led a rough-and-tumble existence. Fun was physical, not cerebral, and boxing was the coolest form of fun. Still, he began to recognize a quiet dignity and intelligence in his mother that would become a beacon to him in many future relationships.

Along with the nuns and Father Curran, Fred and Molly Halle immersed their children in Catholic ritual and thought. The routines of the household provided a strong perception of values and religious observance to the Halle children.

"Until he passed away, my dad always knelt at his bed at night and said prayers. He always did. Mom did too," Bruce Halle remembers. "They were religious people and, according to standards then, they lived that way. We had a beautiful childhood. There were no problems, no fights and no drunkenness, no swearing. It was a beautiful family. I think we were very blessed."

For a boy in grade school, religious instruction is seldom about the intricacies of dogma. Bruce Halle remembers only the generally positive precepts delivered by his parents, Father Curran and the nuns at St.

Kieran's, but the lessons were internalized forcefully in Halle's mind. The simple lessons of common courtesy, the Golden Rule and charity would become a critical source of Halle's lifetime success.

"Even though we had five kids at that time and Dad was just a fireman, we were better off than some of our neighbors," he recalls. "I remember a movie was ten cents and we'd go, but the Hogan family across the street was a bigger family than ours. Mom and Dad would give Fred and Bob and me a dime to go and then, on occasion, they'd give us an extra dime so we could each take a Hogan kid. A dime was a lot in those days."

Catherine Kearns McKelvey, Molly's mother, died after a brief illness in 1937, and was laid out on a bier in the McKelvey house on Third Avenue. The sight of his grandmother unnerved six-year-old Bruce, who spent as much time as he could outside the house, sitting on a sled in the February chill, hoping the ordeal would end soon. His father's mother, Mary, tried to comfort him, but her words had no effect on the frightened boy.

The loss of her mother left Molly as the caretaker of seven men: her own five sons, her husband and, now, her father. While Fred Halle avoided alcohol—keeping a promise he made to Molly when they married—Bruce and his brothers learned about demon rum from their grandfather. John Patrick McKelvey, retired from the paper mill, was an energetic member of the Moose Lodge in Berlin and, too often, an overly enthusiastic participant in their Friday night festivities.

"On Friday nights, he used to go to the Moose Club and he'd come home with too much beer and invariably, Grandpa, going upstairs to the second floor, would fall down," Bruce Halle remembers. "Mom would call us and Fred Jr. and I would go and help Grandpa get up and make sure he made it."

Not yet a teenager, Bruce earned sips of beer from his grandfather in return for simple chores. "My grandfather was the only one in the house that drank," he recalls. "Of course, because of him, I got to have a beer once in a while because I'd help him break his tobacco up for his pipe and he would give me a taste of his beer."

Besides carrying their grandfather upstairs, the boys had more mundane chores. Although there was a pump behind the house on Third

Avenue, Bruce and his brothers were responsible for pulling their wagon, filled with glass containers, up the street to the base of Mount Forist, where a freshwater spring provided clean water for drinking and cooking.

"It was a different time. There were no children challenging the parents," Halle remembers. "Mom and Dad were in charge, they were the bosses, and we were all pretty well-behaved little kids. When necessary, Dad would punish. He'd spank, which was common. He didn't kill us. We all lived. It was a different time, and you didn't challenge your parents. You obeyed."

Of course, Bruce and his brothers didn't always obey. Like most youngsters, they looked for new excitement each day, and Berlin offered more opportunity for exploration and fun than any modern theme park. In addition to the movie theater and the scout troop that Fred Halle and Father Curran led, the boys had Mount Forist.

Mount Forist, two thousand feet high and enticing, stood a few hundred feet beyond the McKelveys' back yard. Although their father and Father Curran would take the boys skiing on the mountain, the strict rule was never to go up on the mountain alone.

"First thing in the morning, Mom and Dad said, 'Don't go up in the mountain,' so that's of course where we went, and we'd pick blueberries," Bruce Halle remembers. "So we'd come back down the mountain and Mom and Dad would know we were there because we had blue tongues and blue lips."

The boys also ignored the strict rules against ringing doorbells and running away on Halloween, hopping on and off the freight trains rolling slowly through town, and walking along the railroad tracks on the way to school. Whenever the boys misbehaved, Molly would direct Fred regarding the appropriate punishment. "Wait until your father gets home" was more than an idle threat.

"Spankings were in the mode then, and my dad knew how to do that, but my brothers and I earned them all, so there was no problem," Bruce Halle says today.

As Halle looks back on his days in Berlin, he remembers simply having a great time. The world was frightening for families who couldn't make ends meet, but life was just plain fun for a boy surrounded by his brothers and friends and a dad who was the most entertaining guy in the world. The Halle boys, including the biggest boy in the pack—Fred Sr.—knew how to have a good time.

As the 1930s drew to a close, Fred's good times—scouting, playing Santa, singing, coaching boxers—kept him away from the house for extended hours. Fred Jr. was gone much of the time as well, seeking part-time jobs. Increasingly, Bruce began to transition into a new role, becoming the man of the house when his father wasn't around.

"Bruce was the one who took over with the children," said his cousin, Charlotte Fournier. "He wasn't the oldest, but he fell into that situation."

Eventually, Bruce's chores came to include dispensing spankings to his younger brothers.

"Other than Dad, I was Mom's rock," Bruce says. "I was there to help her manage the rest of the kids and I used to do that. In fact, I remember having to punish my brothers. I forget what they did, but it doesn't matter. I would do it for Mom. 'Take these kids downstairs and square them away.' It was fair. It didn't hurt them. They survived."

While spankings were doled out on a strictly-business basis, Bruce developed a bad temper as a youngster that took many years to outgrow. People who know the adult Bruce Halle might not recognize the child he had been.

"When I was a kid, I had a terrible temper. I was a little shithead," Halle says now, "and I deserved some of the things I got. I don't know if I was mad about something. I just had a temper."

Bruce and Fred Jr. fought regularly, although the fighting was both a form of competition and a way of having fun. Bruce was younger, but he was large for his age, so the two brothers were evenly matched. As Bruce bested his brother in many of their fights, the competition often grew more severe between the two. Even though the fights got out of hand from time to time, battling between brothers was considered normal, unlike Bruce's bursts of anger with others outside the family.

"I'd just spout off and I'd do things," Bruce remembers. "I hit the girl next door, Doreen Piper, who was my age and a classmate, and one day, for some reason, I slapped her. She went crying home to her parents and her parents told my dad and I learned I shouldn't do that. I never did it again."

While Bruce was overwhelmed at times by his own temper, he and his siblings never recall seeing their father swearing or striking out in anger. Spankings were a job Dad had to do, but Bruce Halle recalls that "it was just business."

At the same time, Fred Halle didn't take crap from anyone, especially when his family was involved. One Christmas, the family was driving out into a wooded area to find a tree to bring home for Christmas. The story has improved with age. The owner of a nearby house was armed with either an axe or a shotgun when he came on to his porch and started swearing at Molly and the children.

"Maybe we were on his property," Bruce Halle guesses. "But he's yelling and swearing at my mother and us just as Dad is coming out of the woods with this Christmas tree that he just chopped down. Dad walked right up to the porch to him. I never heard him say 'damn.' He just didn't. But Dad wouldn't take that from anybody. So Dad goes on up on the porch and hits that guy two or three times and that was the end of that."

In 1939, Fred Halle was promoted to deputy chief of the Berlin Fire Department and life settled into a pleasant pattern for the natural-born entertainer. As the 1940s dawned, though, the family was about to experience another major upheaval, one that would send Bruce and his family into very different worlds.

By December 1941, when the Japanese attack on the U.S. Navy base at Pearl Harbor heralded the beginning of World War II, the Halles had just welcomed their sixth child into the world—Mary Ellen was born earlier that year. As the United States shook off decades of isolationism to confront its new enemies, Congress authorized the conscription of all able-bodied men aged eighteen and older. At thirty-eight years old, Fred thought he might be exempted from the draft as a consequence of having six children to care for, but his hopes were futile. Fred would be drafted and his family would most likely be destitute—relying on cousins and friends in Berlin for basic sustenance.

Just as the McKelvey family had taken the Halles in during the Great Depression, a McKelvey came through again for Fred. A cousin of Molly's worked in the personnel department at Ford Motor Company and Ford was a defense contractor. Civilians employed in critical defense roles could avoid the draft, and Ford's Rouge River plant needed security guards. Fred and his family could stay together through the war, but only if they moved to the Motor City.

Fred Halle packed as much as he could stuff into his old Chevrolet sedan and left Berlin for his new job. Fred Jr., too young to be drafted but old enough to find odd jobs, struck out on his own and would not rejoin the family for more than a year. Bruce, barely a teen, assumed the parental role that would not naturally fall to a second son. As the family prepared to board a train for Detroit, Bruce Halle was the de facto man of the house. It would be his job to keep the rest of the children in line as Molly carried the household six hundred miles from her hometown to the unknown.

BRAVE NEW WORLD

For more than a decade, essentially all of Bruce's life thus far, the Halles had been sheltered by the close network of their extended families in Berlin. Mass at St. Kieran's, the view of Mount Forist from the McKelvey home and even the smell of the paper mills provided the comfortable sense of belonging. Now, that life was ending.

Fred's departure in the family car left Molly and Bruce to cope with the challenges of moving household goods, clothing and four younger children. The Halles had no luggage, but a friend at a local mortuary found some old casket boxes for their household goods. Molly said good-bye to her father, hugged her cousins and boarded the train to her new life, with four sons and a baby girl in tow. A few months after her relocation to Detroit, Molly's father would have a fatal stroke. She would be unable to return to attend the funeral.

The train ride to Detroit was a life-changing experience for Bruce Halle, who was playing the role of dad to his brothers and sister. Mary Ellen, born in 1941, was still in diapers and Molly was pregnant with her last child, Elizabeth Louise, who would be born in Detroit.

Molly and the children stopped overnight in Springfield, Massachusetts, where Fred and Molly had moved shortly after their wedding in 1927. Molly wanted to spend time with Harold and Louise LaFleck, who had befriended the young couple and became Bruce's godparents. While the family was in Springfield, Molly bought Bruce his first pair of slacks, a rite of passage from the overalls and knickers he had been wearing when he was a boy in Berlin. The symbolism of young Bruce, suddenly wearing the pants in the family, was notable.

The move and train ride were an adventure for Bruce, who relished his role as the alpha male in the entourage. As the family collected its possessions and left the train in Detroit, a new world presented itself to a boy whose greatest adventure thus far had been the forbidden Mount Forist. While Berlin was a fair-sized town in 1942, Detroit was already a metropolis. Coming off the train in Detroit was like awakening in the Land of Oz.

"Living in that little town in New Hampshire, I had never seen a black man, I had never seen an alley behind a house, I'd never seen a street car, I'd never seen a building more than three or four stories high," Halle recalls today. "I was a rube from the country, I really was."

Fred had rented a house at Calvary and McMillan on the southwest side of Detroit, just a few blocks from the Holy Redeemer church and school. It was the first time in more than a decade that Fred Halle would be providing the roof over his own household.

Security work at Ford kept Fred out of the army, but it didn't put enough food on the table for a family of eight. Fred took on additional jobs and the family scraped by as each of the older children took on added chores.

"We were a family doing what we could with food stamps—war stamps—and going to the store for my mother," remembers Bob Halle, the third-oldest brother.

The family settled into its traditional patterns in Detroit, with Fred working two or three jobs and Molly finding a way to stretch the budget. As had been the case in Berlin, Bruce also took on the disciplinarian role when Fred wasn't home, which was most of the time. As Fred struggled to keep the family fed, Molly called on Bruce to fill in the gaps.

In Berlin, Bruce could walk with his brothers and father to the fire-house, feeling like a big kid while he carried Fred's lunch pail. At the firehouse, he and his brothers could slide down the pole or climb on the truck. In Detroit, Fred's work was less visible to his adolescent son. Molly's work, however, was starkly apparent as she struggled to manage her over-loaded household. The burden was overwhelming at times. In class one day at Neinas Elementary School, Bruce was setting type in an industrial arts class when he looked out the window and saw his baby sister, Betty, toddling down the street, naked. He dashed out of the building to grab her and bring her home, facing merciless ribbing upon his return to class.

Bruce enrolled in 1944 as a freshman at Holy Redeemer High School, a few blocks from the family's rented home. Bruce settled into the Catholic education system easily, but mixing with other ethnic groups was more challenging in the highly diverse community.

"We'd have disagreements like all kids and we'd have some fights and little mini-gang wars, but not gang wars like today," Halle says. "I remember in little gang wars, we'd have to run and hide from another group chasing us because our group was small at that time, until we got some support. It was just amazing. I remember running into movie theaters and hiding in there and hoping to come out when they're not there and running home. It was just a way of life."

Fitting in was somewhat easier at Holy Redeemer, where Bruce's strength and size proved to be an admission ticket. He joined the foot-ball, basketball and track teams, just as his father had done at Berlin High School, and felt at home as part of the teams. That camaraderie and his comfort with Catholic school tied Bruce closely to Holy Redeemer, which created a new challenge for the family when Fred could finally afford to buy a house.

In 1945, as World War II was coming to a close and the GIs surged home, pent-up demand from the Depression and war years was unleashed and suburbia beckoned. In 1946, Fred Halle found a house for his family at 7750 Huron Street in Taylor Township, about thirteen miles from Detroit. The American Dream of home ownership was finally in reach, if only he could qualify for a mortgage. Again, one of Molly's family members came to the rescue.

"George Jenkins lived not too far from where this new house was and George and his wife, Harriet—she was a cousin of Mom's—helped my mom and dad qualify for a mortgage," Bruce remembers. "He must have cosigned or something like that and we bought this house, which was two blocks away from where they lived."

While the family had grown up together in Berlin and Detroit, the move to Taylor Township would send several of the children on diverging paths. In Berlin, all the Halle children would attend the same grade school and high school. In Taylor Township, which had no high school at the time, the arrangements were more complicated. Ultimately, Bruce, Bob, Jim and Alan would all attend different high schools, as would Fred Jr., who joined the family after a stint in the Merchant Marine and before joining the Marine Corps.

Mary Ellen, still a preschooler when the family moved to Taylor, saw her home life as normal, just as Bruce had described his own life in Berlin. Mom and Dad were quietly religious, leading by example. Dad was seldom home, but he taught Mary Ellen to dance, and they had great fun. Mom kept the house intact and "was the glue that held the family together."

When the family unpacked and settled into their new home, Bruce was beginning his junior year at Holy Redeemer High School. He had made friends on the athletic teams and thrived—socially, if not academically—in the Catholic education system. He wanted to continue at Holy Redeemer and his parents, true believers, were willing to make the investment to keep him there.

In fact, Fred and Molly had thought their third son, Bob, might become a priest. He was studious, quieter than his older brothers and more thoughtful, less instinctive. Taylor Township offered no Catholic high school options, however, and high school was still a year away for Bob, in any event.

"The tuition at Holy Redeemer High School, when you were in parish, was $20 a semester," according to Bruce, but "out of the parish it was $40. That was a lot of money, but my mom and dad paid that and I stayed there. I didn't realize it then, but that might have been one of the most life-changing decisions I ever made."

Getting to school from the family's new home was a logistical challenge. Bruce would walk to the bus stop and catch the bus to the streetcar stop on Fort Street. The streetcar stopped at Junction, about a mile from Holy Redeemer, leaving him to walk the final blocks to school. Hitchhiking was common at the time, and Halle would often thumb a ride to save the dime it cost to take the streetcar.

Like his older brother, Bruce began looking for part-time jobs to help cover his expenses, and he proved to be adept at finding employment. During the course of his high school years, he would find work as diverse as cutting grass at Holy Cross Cemetery, developing film at Cunningham's Drug Store, delivering packages by bicycle at a Kaiser-Frazer car plant and, wearing a blood-stained smock, standing guard behind the meat truck while Molly's cousin, George Moore, made deliveries to grocery stores. The word wasn't in common usage at the time, but Bruce Halle had become something of a schmoozer. In the summer, he applied his skills to find work not only for himself, but for high school friends as well.

Between his classes, athletics and part-time jobs, Bruce was seldom home and, much like his father, sleeping more than awake when he was with his family. One night, sleep deprived and returning from a practice, Bruce fell asleep at the wheel of his father's 1937 Dodge.

"I went off the side of the road and there were telephone poles around me and I swerved," Halle says. "Fenders weren't part of the body, so the right front fender comes off and part of the running board, but it ran. The radiator was broken and I wasn't that far from the house. I got home and dropped the car in front of the house. It's Saturday night. Dad gets up in the morning and goes out to take the rest of the family to church. I'm sleeping and he comes in and wakes me up: 'What happened to the car?' And I told him. He said, 'Did anybody get hurt?' I said, 'No.' He said, 'Okay.' That's all he said. Nobody got hurt."

The car sat in front of the house for weeks while Bruce scraped up the money to have the radiator fixed and his father cadged rides or hitchhiked to work. The car was Fred's mobility and he couldn't afford to replace it, but he didn't really care much. Years later, Bruce would show little emotional attachment to most of his possessions, including cars, as he took his father's example to heart.

"Dad was out of the car for a long while, but he never really said anything else to me about it. His question was, 'Did anybody get hurt?' That's it. Not many people are that calm under those situations and he was terrific that way. I'll never forget that."

THE POLISHED PEOPLE

As the family settled into its normal life in Taylor Township, Bruce Halle became a dual citizen of Taylor and Detroit. Between commuting, sports, school and part-time jobs, Halle was off on his own almost as much as Fred and Fred Jr. Away from family most of the time, he began to notice another part of the world.

"When I was in high school, there were a number of classmates whose parents had a business. There were Terry and Denny McGovern. Their parents had a funeral home right there in the neighborhood, McGovern's funeral home. Then there was a girl and, right there in the neighborhood, her parents had a little potato chip factory. They had a brand name and they packaged them and that kind of thing. I remember thinking how lucky those guys were. Their parents had businesses," Halle remembers.

Similarly, the Kelly brothers at Holy Redeemer came from a family that owned a successful restaurant. While most students would take the street-car to school, the Kelly boys would often drive. "Once in a while I'd get lucky and they'd give me a ride in the car. After football practice when they had the car, we'd pull over to their father's restaurant and we'd go down in the cellar and get a beer. It was so cool. I think the old man probably knew it, but we just went and had one beer and then we went back and showered and went home," Halle says.

Even more impressive than beer in the restaurant basement was a new invention called television. Halle had been listening to boxing matches on radio since he was a child in Berlin, but one of the upperclassmen at the school, Bill DiDonato, had a television set in his home—one of roughly 2,500 television sets in the Detroit area at the time. The cathode ray tube was about the size of the iPad Halle carries today, but the experience of seeing things he could only hear as a child was dramatically exciting for the self-described rube from New Hampshire.

The contrast between people who owned a business and those who merely worked for someone else's company began to etch itself in Halle's mind. "My father was working at the Ford plant, you know, and these people were a different level than we were," he thought.

In Berlin, the Alfred Halle & Son butcher shop was the only example of a family business close to Bruce's life, but his father had left that business behind long before Bruce was born. Bruce had thought his grandfather, Wilfred Halle, was a cool guy and a cut above some of the other adults he met, but he was too young to think of his grandfather in terms of business ownership. In the working-class neighborhoods where the Halles lived in Michigan, everyone worked at the Ford plant—unless they worked for GM. Blue-collar dads raised blue-collar sons. It was that simple.

"Most guys that graduated from high school in Detroit did that," Halle remembers. "They'd become policemen or firemen or went to work in the plants—General Motors, Cadillac, Ford, all of them were there. Those were good jobs."

While good, blue-collar jobs were available in the auto plants and cop houses of Detroit, Halle began to notice that there were other jobs as well. In high school, Bruce started paying attention not only to the people who owned businesses, but also those who were performing more professional, white-collar jobs. One such professional was a neighbor, Carl Hansen, who had learned of Bruce's commute to Holy Redeemer and offered to drive him to school in the mornings.

"I'd get up, and Carl lived a couple of doors down, and I'd just walk down and get in his car, and we'd go to school. It was great," Halle says. "I was lucky. I think that the man had charm and polish and taste. He was a quality guy. He had more education than anybody in my family and he was an engineer," Halle says now. Halle cannot remember what kind of engineer Hansen was, but it was clear there was more career opportunity in the world than working in the car plants. To Halle, Carl Hansen was one of the people who was polished and elegant, a cut above the level that had been the norm for Halle until then.

The rides to work helped Halle win support from some of the nuns at Holy Redeemer. Hansen left for work early in the morning, dropping Halle off outside school ten to fifteen minutes before morning Mass. Halle had nothing else to do at that time of day, so he would sit in the chapel to warm up from the chill. The nuns, though, saw his early arrival as a sign that he was simply one of the more committed Catholics in the school.

While Bruce Halle was discovering the world of people who owned businesses and the "polished people" with white-collar jobs, he also became much more aware of girls. Holy Redeemer had been teaching boys and girls in separate classes since its founding, but classes were combined in the fall of 1944. On the first day of his freshman year, Halle had spotted the girl who would become his wife of thirty-eight years.

"I was near the back and I looked over and in the first row, by the window, in the second seat, is Gerry. I thought she was very cute," Halle says. Geraldine Konfara was several months older than Bruce, just as his own mother was seven months older than his father. Gerry's father worked in the same plant as Fred Halle and the two men knew each other, although they were not social friends. Gerry's background was as working class as Bruce's, but she seemed to have the wiser perspective more prevalent among the polished people.

Bruce and Gerry didn't begin dating until junior year, after his family moved to Taylor, but they got to know each other before then through the Blue Room, a set of high-school dances supervised by the nuns at Holy Redeemer. Gerry was going steady with a student one year older than she, so Bruce's opportunity didn't open up fully until Gerry's beau graduated at the end of their junior year.

Although Bruce and Gerry dated other people during high school and college, Bruce saw something special in Gerry, something that reminded him of his mother. The two were not physically similar, but both seemed to be smarter, more sophisticated, more elegant—"squared away," in Bruce's words.

Bruce Halle never believed he was quite the equal of the elegant, polished people he'd meet from time to time. He saw his mother as a person who could exist comfortably in both worlds, and he thought of Gerry in much the same way.

Halle loved and respected his father and believed in him as a hardworking provider, but he saw his mother as someone who needed and deserved a bit more protection and support than she had received thus far in her life. One Christmas, Bruce saved up a few dollars from his part-time jobs and by hitchhiking to school instead of taking the streetcar, and he bought his mother a purse. Not just a purse. *THE PURSE.* It was leather and it was the nicest purse, possibly the nicest gift, she had ever received.

The experience of giving a gift with so much impact was life-changing for Halle, engendering a lifelong habit of seeking gifts that would create a similar effect with recipients. Halle has given millions of dollars in gifts since then, but the item he speaks of most frequently, and with the greatest pride, is the leather purse he bought for his mom roughly sixty-five years ago.

Halle had learned to enjoy giving rather than receiving, and he had internalized the teachings of his parents and the Church, but the still-immature teenager had yet to shake some of the bad habits that had led him into trouble as a boy. Halle found it fun, from time to time, to catch mice in the cemetery where he cut the grass and release the vermin on the streetcar. Those pranks were minor, however, in comparison to the unpredictable temper that continued to overwhelm Halle at times.

"One time when Fred Jr. was still home, I was at the kitchen table having dinner. Fred was across the table. We're having some bad words," Halle remembers. "There was a roast beef there and there was a knife here, and

I threw the knife at Fred. I was no knife thrower. It just hit him blunt and Dad was sitting there. Dad was a pretty big man and he just went *whap* to me and I went flying into the other room, chair spinning over."

The aggression between brothers—almost always Bruce and Fred Jr.—was an ongoing story in the Halle household. Their competition became decidedly more public in 1948, when the two man-boys met for The Fight.

Nobody, including Bruce Halle, can quite explain the circumstances that led to the final confrontation between Fred Halle's two oldest sons. The Battle of Huron Street was a grudge match, to be sure, but it's not clear what the grudge was about or when it was over.

From the beginning, in Berlin, Fred Jr. and Bruce stood in awe of their father's pugilistic dexterity. Fred Halle was bigger than life to the boys and nothing made him quite so big as his boxing talents. He taught his sons to box at an early age and, even at the preteen level, Bruce and Fred Jr. had developed a substantial rivalry. As is the case with most brothers, there was both love and hate involved.

In high school, Bruce helped his brother push their father's car down the street so Fred Jr. could go for a joy ride with friends without his dad hearing the car start. When Fred Jr. married outside the Catholic faith, Fred and Molly would not attend the wedding in a Methodist Church, but Bruce and Bob traveled down to Owensboro, Kentucky to stand up with their brother.

Although his parents were dismayed, Bruce took a more pragmatic view of his brother's choice. "That marriage was such a 'disaster' that Fred and Jane were married for fifty years before Jane passed away," he says with a smile.

Coexisting with the unbreakable bond between the brothers, the battle for boxing supremacy remained an open wound. In 1948, Fred Halle Jr. came home from the Marine Corps to visit his family in Taylor Township. Bruce was a senior at Holy Redeemer High School, still stronger than his older brother, but Fred Jr. had been boxing in the Marines and won his division championship at Parris Island. At home, trash talk turned into a challenge and the battle was joined.

"He kicked the shit out of me," Bruce Halle admits.

The brothers put on their gloves and began fighting in the backyard. Bruce was bigger, but Fred Jr. was much faster and more agile. For every punch Bruce landed, Fred Jr. countered with three or four. The fighting continued in the backyard, then the front yard, and neighbors gathered to watch as Fred Jr. and Bruce thrashed their way across the street. The women stopped watching, disgusted by the violence, but the men stared at the unfolding armageddon.

Finally, in the vacant lot across the street, the brothers ended up on the ground, wrestling and throwing more punches. "I'm bleeding and it finally ends up as a wrestling match, and I get Fred on the ground and blood is pouring out of my nose and it's filling his eye sockets. That drove him crazy."

It's not completely clear which man ended the fight, but it was definitely agreed that Fred Jr. was the winner.

"One of his goals was to come back and beat the shit out of his little brother and he did. He did a good a job of it, too," Bruce Halle remembers. "It was fun. It was a great match and we talked about that for years afterwards and it was good. It was part of family and part of growing up with a bunch of boys in that time frame."

Flush with victory, Fred Jr. moved on to a greater challenge: Fred Halle Sr. Big mistake.

"Dad was a better boxer than me, and he was a faster and bigger man than Fred. So they're fighting in the kitchen and Fred couldn't match Dad and Dad finally said, 'That's enough of that.' He hits Fred in the chest really hard and Fred goes through the door and lands on the steps going down. He broke the door and my mother wanted to kill my father. Dad didn't know which way to hold a screwdriver, so I said, 'Mom, I'll fix it. I'll fix it.' She was going to kill those two guys."

Fred Jr. proved his point to Bruce. Fred Sr. proved his point to Fred Jr. Nobody died. The end. For Bruce Halle, recollections of The Battle of Huron Street fit into the pattern of most memories. If it was a good experience, it was neat or cool. If the experience was challenging, it was just the way things were. Strictly business. As that way of thinking would become the norm over time, Halle would establish a leadership style that would be highly attractive to thousands of followers.

In 1948, the year of the fight and Halle's graduation from Holy Redeemer, the world was not quite so orderly. As Bruce graduated and prepared to begin college, Fred's earnings from multiple jobs proved inadequate for the still-packed household.

Molly and Fred helped Bruce with his college expenses and both Bruce and Bob would ultimately complete college on the GI Bill, but the family finances offered less opportunity for Fred and Molly's other children. As Bruce left for college, Molly left home each day to earn a living.

"I was fortunate. My mother had to go to work later and that had a big effect on my brothers and sisters. Up until the time that I graduated high school, Mom didn't have to go to work," Halle remembers.

Molly's first job, working in a cafeteria at a car plant, was not the best fit, but office work proved to be a good match for the socially adept, though quiet, mother of seven. Molly's math skills were of significant value in an office environment and she proved to be an excellent employee. Still, in the late 1940s, a working wife was not a positive reflection on a husband as the provider to a family.

"I can't look at my dad as a failure," Bruce says, "but it was sad that my mother had to go to work for many years." Bruce was influenced strongly by the daily challenges his mother faced. Even if he didn't know it yet, he was determined that that his own wife would have a better life than his mom's.

Returning to the workforce was not the final challenge for Molly, however. Fred's mother moved to Michigan after her husband died, taking up residence with Fred's sister, Stella Hughes. When the family matriarch visited the Halle home on Huron Street, the old French-Canadian widow enjoyed conversing with her son—in French.

"In the house, when we lived in Michigan, Grandma would talk French to Dad and Dad would, of course, answer his mother," Halle remembers. Intentionally, the conversations were indecipherable to Molly, the Irish girl who had stolen Frederick J. Halle from his family back in Berlin.

THE SPEECH

Bruce Halle's horizons expanded as he completed his education at Holy Redeemer High School. As he adapted to his new surroundings, he learned to survive in a cauldron of feuding ethnic groups and find jobs to bring in the spare change essential to any teenager's life. Meeting people whose parents owned a business, he recognized a path to prosperity he had never known of in Berlin. Riding to school with Carl Hansen, he considered the doors that could open for a man with a bit of the elegance and class Bruce had yet to attain. Looking at Gerry and at his own mother, he realized there were people who could cross over from his world into the world of the polished people, a world where he wouldn't quite fit without a passport or a guide.

None of these thoughts was a burning notion at the time. It would be simplistic to suggest that the teen's exposure to different types of people lit an all-consuming passion that drove him to success. Still, a small flame had been lit, a flame that would grow.

Despite all the options he saw as he looked around his expanding universe, one critical piece was missing. Halle was a good athlete, but not a great one. He was a passable student, in the literal sense of that term, but he recognized himself as forty-ninth runner-up for valedictorian in a class of fifty. He got along well with most people, when his temper didn't derail him, but he wasn't a natural leader.

While he could see that other people had found paths to great success—from owning businesses to professional careers—he didn't see any of those paths leading to success for Bruce Thomas Halle.

Sister Marie Ellen provided that vision.

Sister Marie Ellen belonged to the Immaculate Heart of Mary order that had taken over responsibility for educating all students at Holy Redeemer High School in Bruce Halle's freshman year. The order was founded in 1845 in Monroe, Michigan, by Father Louis Gillet and Sister Theresa Maxis, and Holy Redeemer Parish opened its high school in 1897. For more than four decades, boys and girls attended separate schools. The Immaculate Heart of Mary sisters taught the girls and the Brothers of Mary taught the boys. In 1944, Bruce Halle's freshman year, the Brothers of Mary left the school and classes were combined.

On his first day of class in 1944, Bruce met two of the people who would influence his life the most: Geraldine Konfara, his future wife, and Sister Marie Ellen, his homeroom teacher. Sister Marie Ellen saw more in Halle than he saw in himself, and she shared that view with him in a way that changed him forever.

As Bruce would move on in his life, he'd meet several people who saw promise in him, from the person who would lend him money for his wedding to the mentor who lent him money to invest in his first (failed) business and the first distributors to open a line of credit for his fledgling tire company. Over the ensuing years, Halle would make sure he repaid the confidence people showed in him, both financially and ethically. Each of his patrons would learn that their faith in Halle was justified, that he could be trusted to deliver on his promises.

Before all of them, however, there was Sister Marie Ellen.

"She had faith in me," Halle remembers simply.

Sister Marie Ellen was one of the many people with a better vocabulary and social skills than Halle possessed, which made her opinion of him credible, albeit surprising. As his final semester began, Bruce Halle needed two half-credits to graduate with the rest of his class. While Sister Rose worked with Halle to complete his biology requirements, Sister Marie Ellen began tutoring him in English.

As Halle struggled to perfect his writing skills, Sister Marie Ellen began to ask him about his plans for the future. Like many of his classmates, Halle had a vague idea about graduating and finding a job, possibly in an auto plant. The nun suggested college as an alternative path.

"My high school academic record would make you think I wasn't smart enough," Halle says with a smile. "I have those records and, once in a while when I really feel like punishing myself, I look at them. It's terrible."

Even more startling than Sister Marie Ellen's vision of Bruce Halle as a college student was her suggestion that he give a graduation address on behalf of his fellow athletes. Halle was comfortable and engaging in small groups, but he had never made any kind of public presentation. When he had moved to Detroit, his New England accent was a source of humor for many of his classmates, who thought he sounded sarcastic if all he said was "hello." By the time he was a senior at Holy Redeemer, the accent had not softened much, but he wonders if it had become more endearing as the faculty got to know him better. Whatever the case, Sister Marie Ellen changed the course of his life with a simple suggestion that he speak in public.

"I probably wouldn't have gone to college. I don't know what I was going to do," Halle remembers. "But she inspired me to do something different, because I would have probably taken a job in Detroit like my classmates."

Certainly, the suggestion of a college education wouldn't come from Halle's parents. Higher education was a foreign concept to his working-class father, and the costs seemed insurmountable. Even more relevant, Bob was the smarter son, the better student, and he would naturally be the first to go to college if any Halle son made that leap.

But Bruce Halle, not Bob, was the son who was graduating this particular year, and his homeroom teacher was showing more faith in him than he had in himself. Sister Marie Ellen worked with him through the spring months, helping him earn his missing half credit in English and draft his speech. As they worked together on class work, preparing the presentation and rehearsing Halle's delivery, the idea of college became increasingly less strange.

"We started in February or March, and I was spending a lot of time with her after class and during class or after school, writing this talk and then practicing it and having her help me," Halle says. "I spent a lot of time with her, and obviously she was an intelligent school teacher and she just inspired me. Okay, I am going to go to college. I'm going to go to Eastern. I'm going to go. Actually, three of my classmates went and I roomed with them. Of course, I think they were all surprised I joined them, but I did."

Halle's speech was titled "The American Way of Life," and it marked his first public speaking opportunity. His audience was on his side, though, as the C-minus student exhorted them to "Take your diploma, and with it your ambitions. Keep your ideals close to your heart, and with your youth and energy go forth into this land and make your dreams come true. For this is America, the land of opportunity."

The exact text of the speech was not wholly relevant, because the experience was much more than a teenager's oration. The simple fact of the speech—Sister Marie Ellen's surprising faith that he could be more than he realized—was the life-changing component. Five decades later, in 2001, Halle would return to Holy Redeemer to speak at the dedication of the Halle Gymnasium—a gift from a grateful, though challenged, student.

In the spring of 1948, however, Halle could not predict anything beyond graduation. All he knew then was that there was a bigger world than the one he had grown up in, and an educated, smart, polished woman believed he might have a place in that world.

A FEW GOOD MEN

As Bruce Halle graduated and set his sights on college, business was the furthest thing from his mind. Although he'd been exposed to business people and families that owned businesses while he was in high school, he hadn't ratcheted up his own vision of the possibilities ahead.

Halle enrolled in the fall of 1948 at Michigan State Normal College in Ypsilanti—renamed Eastern Michigan University in 1959—with a goal of becoming a physical education teacher at the high school level. "Coming out of high school and being involved in sports, that's what young guys wanted to do," he explains.

The pressure was substantial for the first Halle to go to college. Fred Jr. had essentially become self-supporting at sixteen, but Bruce continued to rely on his parents for some of his expenses.

"I did most of it and they helped me where they could. Mom and Dad, on the weekend, would give me four or five dollars. That was all that they could do. In fact, it was a big sacrifice at the time and more than I could have expected," Halle says.

Bruce picked up odd jobs to help cover his tuition of $75 per year and living expenses on campus. Working in the cafeteria at the Men's Union gave Halle a chance to forage for food for himself and his friends, but the leftover sandwiches were never quite filling enough for the starving college students. Halle and his roommates at Munson Hall—all friends from Holy Redeemer—would cadge food from young women they knew, including Geraldine Konfara, by writing letters home, all of thirty miles from Ypsilanti to Detroit.

"We wrote to all the girls and gave them a sad story and asked them to send us cookies and stuff like that. Some would actually make cookies and send them, but Gerry worked at J.L. Hudson, so she'd just buy some and send it in a big box and we'd get them that way," Halle says.

Halle continued courting Gerry, and she would often come up to the school for the Saturday-night dances that were a monthly feature of campus social life. During his freshman year in college, Bruce and Gerry attended the wedding of Bill DiDonato—whose family's television had been a source of wonder for Halle in high school—and his bride, Ann. That night, Halle explained to Gerry that the two of them would be married one day, but she scoffed at the idea, and his profession of love didn't turn the two of them into an exclusive couple.

At college, Bruce resumed the patterns of his high school years, including both athletic activities and poor grades. He joined the football team and made friends on the squad, but the combination of work, classes and athletics was more than he could juggle. His grade point average was below C and it was beginning to seem that Sister Marie Ellen was wrong about him, after all.

Halle's college career was interrupted—some might say mercifully—by the start of the Korean War in the summer of 1950. Fred Jr. had enlisted in the Marine Corps Reserve after his stint with the Marines, and Bob Halle decided to enlist as well—even though Bob was still in high school. Both brothers were activated in the summer of 1950, between Bob's junior and senior years in high school, and Bruce felt compelled to enlist as well.

"Now, they're both activated, and I'm ending my sophomore year in college and I'm a failure as a student. I'm not really doing anything, and so I decide to enlist in the Marine Corps," Halle says.

Bruce went to boot camp at Parris Island in South Carolina, while Bob was shipped to San Diego. The two brothers went through boot camp in parallel and compared notes—just a bit competitively—on their progress. Bob remembers besting Bruce's marksmanship score of 209 by setting a record at 210—although he suspects Bruce remembers the scores just a bit differently.

Boot camp was a life-changing experience for Halle, as the combination of training and discipline chipped away at his anger-management challenges. During one touch football game on pavement, a fellow Marine tripped Halle, leaving a bloody scar on his hand. The sergeant allowed Halle to take his revenge, but only for a limited time. When it was time to stop, he had to have the control to stop.

Gaining that control was far from an instant process, but the discipline and force of basic training were more powerful than Halle's temper. Halle began to become more disciplined and, if not less aggressive, certainly more controlled.

"The best piece of advice I ever got in my life, I got from my brother Fred," Halle says. "I was going into the Marine Corps and he told me, 'Bruce, keep your eyes and ears open and your mouth shut.' With his great advice I went into boot camp, and Sergeant Delio, a tech sergeant, is in charge. Sergeant Pratt, a three striper, is his assistant. So they get a new guy in, a Corporal Riley, a reservist that's called up. First day, he takes us to the dentist. In boot camp you can't speak to anybody. You can say, 'Sir, Private Halle requests permission to speak, Sir.' 'Permission granted, speak.' You have to do that. They beat that into you, that whole concept. Now, we're at the dentist, waiting, and I've got to go to the head. So, I walk up to Corporal Riley and I say, 'Corporal, can I go to the head?' That's all. I don't say 'Sir.'

"Later we're in our barracks. Chow is over and I hear: 'Halle, get your ass in here.' They're all in there—Corporal Riley, Sergeant Pratt, Sergeant

Delio—and I'm standing at attention. 'Sir, Private Halle reporting.' Pratt shoved me. I bounced back. He shoved me again. He shoved me some more. Delio, the staff sergeant says, 'Would you like to hit Sergeant Pratt?' 'Yes, sir, fucking right,' I said. So they beat me around, they shoved me around and I survived, but I deserved it. So, in the morning, we fall out and they say, 'Halle, fall out.' I say, 'Oh shit, they're going to kill me here in front of these eighty guys.' But they moved me up to squad leader. Because I took their shit."

After boot camp, Bruce was sent to Camp Lejeune, North Carolina, where Fred Jr. was already a sergeant in a different battalion.

"I go to see Fred, and Fred's a tough dude," Halle says. "All the guys are saying, 'Don't mess with Sergeant Halle.' He's a staff sergeant. I'm a private. I go in the barracks looking for him. 'Don't go looking for him. He's an SOB. Don't go near him.' I walk up to Fred. He's in the hallway and I touch him on the back of the shoulder and he turns around and swings at me. Of course, I knew he was going to do that and I stopped his punch and he says, 'Oh. Bruce.'

"So there was an NCO club, a non-commissioned officers club. I'm a private. I can't go there. But Fred takes me in there and we're getting—it's called a slop shoot there in the Marine Corps, so we're in the slop shoot, getting 3.2 beer. While I'm standing with Fred, out comes the master sergeant that's the head of my company. He kicked me out and he gave Fred hell, but we were brothers and it was fun."

As boot camp ended in November, 1950, the newly promoted private first class enjoyed a thirty-day leave to return home before fulfilling his three-year obligation, which would likely include a tour in Korea. Halle was dating both Gerry and another woman at the time. Although he and Gerry were somewhat a couple and he had predicted that they would marry, they still were not exclusive.

"I had a date with another girl I was dating the first night I got back," Halle remembers. "The second night, I had a date with Gerry. I never went back to the other girl. It was just meant to be with us."

Bruce and Gerry got engaged at the close of 1950, but they debated whether to get married right away or wait until Bruce's military hitch was over. In February 1951, Gerry and another woman traveled to Washington, DC to spend a weekend with Halle and a friend. The couple chose to accelerate their plans and get married the following month, on March 17—St. Patrick's Day.

"Gerry and I are going to get married," Halle remembers. "We have no money and, of course, our families are regular working families. And we're trying to plan a wedding, which we did in Dearborn Heights at Warren Valley Golf Club. The whole thing would cost $800, which was a fortune; I'm a private in the Marine Corps and I'm making $18 a month, something like that. Gerry's cousin, John Van Brunt, was working for a leather maker named Raymond Walk. And Raymond Walk, through John, loaned Gerry and me the $800 to get married and to have this wedding."

In the 1950s, it was common to give the bride and groom the most versatile of gifts: cash. Bruce and Gerry spent their first night of wedded bliss as most newlyweds do: counting the proceeds from their party.

"We are counting it out, because it was a fortune for us, and we got $1,300," Halle beams. "That was amazing."

The newlyweds received a large number of $20 bills at their wedding and, for a working-class family, $20 was a substantial gift. Even after repaying Walk for the $800 loan, Bruce and Gerry started out with $500 in the bank. Later, Halle would decide to give each Discount Tire employee who gets married a gift of $1,000, which he estimates as the modern equivalent of the $20 bills he received in 1951.

Halle had almost missed his wedding, thanks to his inability to secure enough leave time to get from Camp Lejeune to Detroit and back. Halle originally wrangled a one-week pass for his wedding and honeymoon, but the captain cut his leave to seventy-two hours just before his leave was to begin. Lacking the heart—or courage—to break the news to Gerry, Halle left camp and hoped he could get an extension while on the road.

Hitchhiking was a fairly common form of transport in the 1950s and a young Marine in uniform could rely on the kindness of passing motorists. Halle hitched the eight hundred miles from Camp Lejeune to Detroit, arriving just in time for his wedding rehearsal on Friday night. Following his wedding on Saturday, the newlyweds took Gerry's brother's car on their honeymoon to Chicago, with Bruce stopping regularly to call his father for news about a leave extension. The Marine Corps was unrelenting. Halle's leave ended at midnight Sunday.

Bruce and Gerry took a two-day honeymoon in Chicago before driving back to Detroit on Tuesday. Back in uniform, thumb raised, Halle started hitchhiking his way back to Camp Lejeune, arriving on Wednesday—three days overdue. The captain was not amused.

Halle was called into the colonel's office, along with the captain and Halle's master sergeant, who delivered the same advice Halle had received earlier from his older brother—keep your eyes and ears open and your mouth shut. Believing his cause to be just, Halle ignored "the best piece of advice I ever got in my life." His pleadings won him thirty days of mess duty—KP—and the enmity of his commanding officer.

While the punishment ended the matter for the colonel, the captain had unfinished business with his AWOL private and had him transferred to a unit deploying for maneuvers in Europe. With D-Day less than seven years in the past, potential invasions and military exercises had serious meaning for the Marine Corps. For the locals in the Mediterranean nations Halle invaded—Italy, Spain and Greece among them—the show was highly entertaining. Clad in full battle gear, Halle and his fellow Marines would clamber down rope ladders off their ship and into landing barges. As the barges reached shore, the invading horde would leap out to storm the beach while families lazed on nearby picnic blankets, clapping and cheering for the brave young Americans coming to save them.

COMING OF AGE

Maneuvers in Europe separated the newlyweds but provided Bruce Halle a reprieve before he shipped out to Korea. Upon returning to Camp Lejeune in November 1951, Halle was promoted to corporal and received a thirty-day leave to visit the wife he hadn't seen since his two-day honeymoon nine months earlier. They reconnected with family, friends and each other, lunched at J.L. Hudson's department store and tried to fit in enough togetherness to last through their next separation.

On January 1, 1952, Halle took his first plane ride on the way to Camp Pendleton, California and, eventually, Korea. Halle's decision to fly gave him an unexpected break when he reported to his base. When his plane landed at Chicago's Midway Airport—then the world's busiest—a winter storm blocked his progress. Halle reported to base late, along with dozens of other Marines who were stuck on buses, trains or roadside hitchhiking locales. Overdue sergeants were busted to corporal, corporals were busted to private, but Corporal Bruce Halle had a note from the airline and escaped punishment, receiving a promotion to sergeant a few weeks later.

By the time Halle shipped out in early 1952, much of the worst action was over, although his brother, Bob, had not been so fortunate. Bob Halle arrived in Korea in 1951 and was wounded twice in battle—first suffering a minor mortar wound and later a head wound sustained during a nighttime firefight. The family was notified that Bob was missing in action, learning later that he had been found. Bruce Halle's younger brother returned home to Taylor Township at the end of 1951, a war hero.

"I was very fortunate in that I got to Korea in February of 1952," Halle says now. "The end of 1950 is when the United States got chased out of the Chosin Reservoir and I missed that. That was where a lot of guys lost their lives or got hurt. I got there after that."

Still, Korea continued to be a hot war—no peace treaty has ever ended it officially—and Halle's rifle company operated close to the truce line at the 38th parallel.

"We were on the main line of resistance, and we were shooting at people and they were shooting at us, trying to blow us out, and we were trying to blow them out," Halle says. "But we weren't trying to move them further north, and they weren't trying to move us further south. It was just a standoff all that time. So, there was artillery and mortar and some rifle fire, but not much direct contact."

Along the line of the truce, Sergeant Halle's rifle company was assigned to replace the Republic of Korea Army at the forward posts—essentially small bunkers spread across the demilitarized zone. Halle's squad was in the middle, and none of the other bunkers was visible from their location.

"There were only thirteen of us. I was there for thirty days," Halle recalls now. "About a week or ten days after we got there, the position next to ours was overrun. I went over there and the guys were all gone. Their boots were lying there and their clothes. They were taken out of there in the middle of the winter and they took them away. I'll never know what happened to them."

The first night in the forward post, Halle and his squad made a near-fatal error. "There was a fire pit and some logs there. Now this was good, we thought. So we started a fire and we're putting more logs on the fire and we were sitting around and we're thinking, this is not so bad, and then *PING PING PING*, they're shooting at us. They couldn't really see us, exactly, but they were shooting at the fire. Well, they know we're there," he remembers. "Who else but dumb Americans would build a big bonfire there? So, needless to say, we didn't have any more fires."

Potshots from the enemy and the capture of another position reminded the squad that this was a real war zone, so Halle and his men increased their defenses. They set up booby traps of trip wires and hand grenades, tin cans and flares. North Koreans couldn't surprise them, but rats were another story.

"We're lying in the bunker—it was too shallow to stand up—and a big rat ran across my sleeping bag and then across the next guy. Then the rat ran across the third guy's face and he's all shook up and mad and he's got a 45. And *BOOM, BOOM, BOOM*, the rats are running around and *BOOM, BOOM, BOOM*, he's trying to kill the damn things and never did," Halle says. "After that, everybody is awake, everybody is alert.

"The rats, by the way—we'd have a candy bar or a piece of bread and we'd wake up in the morning, and the rats had been chewing on all of them," he continues. "So you'd take your knife and you'd cut out the part they'd bitten and we'd eat the rest of it. That was life in the big city."

Halle found time to pray, as most men in uniform will do, as he considered the fragility of his position. "I never got hurt, but I had some close ones, some very close ones," he recalls. Halle's close encounters paled in comparison to one member of his squad's, who had an uncanny knack for drawing mortar fire every time he ventured to the latrine. "Every time Corporal Pierce went to the head, everyone would say, "Get ready for artillery." It was almost destined; he'd go take a crap and artillery would start coming. You remember the funny things."

Halle's first child, Bruce Jr., was born in September 1952, while Halle was in the line of fire in Korea. Brother Bob, recuperating from his wounds in Michigan, had picked up a letter from Fred and Molly to their son in uniform. On the way to the mailbox, Bob scrawled "It's a boy" on the back of the envelope and sent it on its way. Bruce Jr. would be six months old before he met his father.

Halle returned to the States in February 1953, arriving by troop ship in San Francisco and catching a flight to Detroit for a reunion with his family—his wife of nearly two years and their infant son, his parents and the Konfaras. Sgt. Halle had eight months left in the service, but the war was behind him.

Halle returned to Camp Lejeune much older and wiser than when he had boarded his first plane a year earlier. Still physically fit, he was far more mentally disciplined than he had been when he enlisted at the age of twenty.

At the base in North Carolina, Halle won a promotion to first sergeant, leading 250 enlisted men, including Sergeant Shipkey—"the toughest Marine I ever knew." Halle had the good fortune to be one of the men who picked up a truck that had rolled over on Shipkey in Korea—Shipkey was too tough to be injured, of course—and now he was serving under Halle.

"Now I'm the first sergeant and he's the gunnery sergeant. He's the working sergeant and I'm the head office guy," Halle explains. "When you fall out there in the morning, there's 250 guys who roll out to roll call and they're going to work on me. But I've got Shipkey standing next to me. They aren't going to fuck with me. I was the luckiest guy in the world."

Halle had gained a deeper sense of people, of trust, and of honor during his time in the service. Always a religious person, he began to see how acts of kindness played out in a more intense environment, and he sought to apply the lessons he learned in his new role as a leader.

"One of the guys, a private, had gotten into a tango with a sergeant who I knew was still working there," Halle recalls. "The private had done some brig time and gotten a dishonorable discharge. Well, the MPs bring him to the office and I'm in charge there now and they've got this private and he wants to kill the sergeant, and the sergeant is there. I told the private, 'I've got these two MPs here and you're discharged. You're getting out. Now I can have them march you out the front gate or I can just dismiss them and let you walk out like a man—if you don't go see that sergeant. Don't go talk to him. Just walk out like a man or I'll have them march you out. Which would you like to do?' He says, 'I'll walk out, Sir, like a man.' I let the MPs go. He did go out that way, but the sergeant was terrified that this kid was going to kill him. He talked with me and he said, 'How did you do that?' But it was just a matter of respect, treating people right."

Halle mustered out in September 1953 and returned to Michigan, where he found a job assembling starters and other car parts at Ford's Rawsonville plant in Ypsilanti and enrolled again at Michigan Normal. Although he had set his sights on becoming a physical education instructor when he first enrolled in 1948, Halle now was determined to focus on a business degree. The successful people he'd met were in business of some sort, and he wanted to be a success.

"When I came back from the Marine Corps and went back to college, I was a different person than before, when I went to school to begin with. I had been a terrible student. I didn't apply myself before. I came back after three years in the Marine Corps and I'm an adult. I have grown up. I'm a man," Halle remembers. "I'm not a little boy going to college out of high school. I'm married. We have a baby. It's a whole different world and I'm working in a plant. It's just a whole different world. It's a growing up time. It's when you finally . . . some little light goes on in the back of your head: 'Get your shit together now.'

"It does happen and it's one of the things that I think, danger aside—I think all young men should go into the service. They should go in and get their discipline and get their training and then come back out and start a life somewhere. Most people that you know that have been in the service, injuries aside, they're much better people than they were before."

The newlyweds—plus two years—set up housekeeping in subsidized housing at Willow Run Village in Ypsilanti, Michigan. Rent was $40 per month and electricity was another dollar, but it was still challenging to make ends meet. Halle worked five or six days at the plant and carried a full-time load of classes, adjusting to a work schedule that would serve him well, years later, as the owner of a retail store. Bruce left home at 7:00 a.m. for an 8:00 a.m. class, left school at 2:00 p.m. for a 3:00 p.m. shift at the plant and returned home after 11:00 p.m., only to repeat the same pattern the next day.

Halle's work schedule and the challenges of family life wreaked havoc on his academic performance. By the end of the 1953–54 school year, his grades were well below a C average, and Halle was *persona non grata* at Michigan Normal.

"Unbeknownst to me, the university had decided I was not going to be allowed to register, but I didn't know that, so I got registered," Halle says. "I'm in class, in summer school, and the dean of men calls me. He says I wasn't supposed to register and I have to leave. Then the dean of irregular programs said I could stay if I quit work and attended school full-time. I told him that would be fine if he would support my family. Finally, we agreed that if I got at least a B in my two summer school classes, I could stay."

Halle had nearly missed his high school graduation because he needed more credits in biology and English, and he was taking summer school courses in the same two subjects. He pushed himself hard to get a B in biology but struggled with the interpretive reading class—essentially poetry—that he took with two friends, fellow veterans Dick Adams and Jerry McNally. Halle got lucky again as the teacher had a soft spot for men who had served in uniform.

"Mrs. Best was the teacher and she was a single, mature lady, and the story was that her lover got killed in World War II and he was the love of her life and she never got married again," Halle recalls. "So what Dick and Jerry and I did, all the poems that we would read would be war stories, blood, guts and killing and all that stuff. Now, I had picked up malaria in Korea and then, that summer, I had a little relapse. No big deal. All I did was walk to the Veterans Hospital right there outside Ypsilanti and get a few quinine pills and then come back. Well, I missed class the day before and Mrs. Best asked where I was. So Dick and Jerry tell her I got malaria in the war in Korea and I'm out to the hospital and they made it a big story. When I came back the next day, I felt good, but she says, 'Bruce, put your head down and relax on the table.' I'd put my head down and doze off and she didn't care."

Halle scored a B in biology and an A in the English class, winning a needed reprieve as a student. Michigan Normal welcomed him back as a junior in the fall of 1954.

Despite the discipline of the Marine Corps and the demands of his job and family, Halle hadn't given up on the pranks that provided an extra spark in his life. Halle and three fraternity brothers at Alpha Gamma Epsilon decided it would be funny to kidnap Dick Adams, who had helped him with his English class and was also the president of the fraternity. Halle and his co-conspirators arrived at Adams's home one evening with a master plan—grab Dick, drive him out to the country and leave him there. The plot unraveled, though, as Dick resisted, his wife began beating Bruce with a broom, and a sheriff's car rolled up in the midst of the melee. At the Washtenaw County Jail, the lieutenant looked them up and down, listened to their story and asked them how old they were. When Bruce answered that he was twenty-five, the lieutenant suggested that he give some thought to growing up—then let him go.

In fact, Halle was fully determined to grow up as he shifted his focus to business administration, along with kidnapping co-conspirator Dave Fairbanks. Bruce had reconnected recently with Fairbanks, whom he'd met in an English class when both started school and who also took time out to enlist in the Korean War. Fairbanks was planning to teach accounting in high school and would ultimately become a high school principal—before joining Halle's young company in 1966.

"Bruce was always an outgoing individual, one that people could become easily attracted to," says Fairbanks, now retired and a golf course owner in Michigan's Upper Peninsula. Fairbanks remembers that Halle found his niche in classes on salesmanship and the principles of business. "When he was in some of the college classes, I can think of one in particular, if the professor wasn't sure about an answer, he would call on Bruce," Fairbanks recalls.

In spite of his aptitude for business classes and his ability to make friends, Halle was far behind the pace he needed to graduate after four years of schooling. In 1956, eight years after he enrolled at Michigan Normal for the first time, Bruce Halle earned his degree, a bachelor's of business administration. Bob Halle, two years younger and also a Korea veteran, had nearly caught up with his brother, graduating just a few months later from the same school.

Bruce Halle was the first person in his family to graduate from college and, despite the challenges of finally earning his degree, he believes he could not have been a success without that start. Today, Discount Tire provides a $5,000 annual college scholarship to any child of a full-time employee with three years at the company, along with smaller grants to other students.

"I encourage everybody: 'Go to college. Go to college. Get your degree,'" Halle notes. "One thing that happens, once you get your education and get your degree, that's yours. No one can take that from you. Some things in life in the future might go bad and you could lose a lot, or most, or all of your worldly possessions, but no one is ever going to take that college degree from you, that education. It's there. It's yours forever."

Earning a degree was repayment to Sister Marie Ellen for her confidence and to Halle's parents for their spiritual and financial support. But a degree is only a passport, not a free pass, to success. Bruce Halle, college graduate, was about to take several detours on the road to prosperity.

FALSE STARTS

As Bruce Halle struggled to complete his college education and put food on the table for his family, work in the auto plants presented a dead end that had trapped many members of his high school class.

While he was most conscious of the changes in discipline and focus that he'd gained in the Marine Corps, Halle's strongest capability was his interpersonal skills. Halle had learned how to find jobs for himself and for friends in high school, how to negotiate a second chance from the deans in college and how to win the support of several polished people he'd met along the way.

In the work environment at the Ford plant, though, Halle would realize no benefit from his education or his ability to meet people, make friends and earn their trust. As he cast about for alternative ways to make a living, Bruce remembered a couple he and Gerry knew socially. Bruce knew that the husband sold cars. More than that, the husband was making a very good living selling cars. And if he could do it, why couldn't Bruce T. Halle, soon-to-be college graduate?

In the fall of 1955, Halle, still a college student, began walking down dealership row on Michigan Avenue in Ypsilanti, offering car dealers his personality, energy and decidedly unproven talent. Employing the same skills that had landed jobs for him and his friends in school, Halle convinced Harry Regetz, general manager of a DeSoto Plymouth dealership, to give him a try—no salary, straight commission. Halle gave his two-week notice at the Ford plant.

When he returned to the dealership to begin working, however, Regetz was no longer general manager. He'd been demoted to the used car lot and the new general manager, Fred Johnson, had never heard of Bruce Halle or Regetz's offer. Johnson relented and gave Halle the same deal he'd received from Regetz: Halle would make no money until he sold a car.

Under pressure to produce, Halle quickly expanded his prospecting well beyond the showroom and personal acquaintances. He would spot a dilapidated car on the road and write down the license plate number. Then, Halle would check the registration of the vehicle, which was an open record at the time, and pay the owner a visit at home. As he developed his pitch and success level, Halle moved on to his next dealership, John Barbour Ford, where his fraternity president and friend, Dick Adams, was already on the sales team.

"I'd have a customer there and I'd be having a difficult time closing and so I'd say, 'Excuse me. Let me go get Mr. Barbour and see if he could help us here.' Dick would come out and I would introduce him as Mr. Barbour. 'What are you doing here? Can I help you?' And he would do the same thing. He'd introduce me as Mr. Barbour and we'd move in to close the deal. We were pretty slick guys. We were having fun. And, we were making good money," Halle remembers. That type of shenanigans would get a man fired at Discount Tire today, but Halle's business philosophy was still somewhat more flexible than it would be in later years.

Working on commission provided the big payoffs that laboring in the auto plants couldn't offer to the young father. As he'd complete one transaction, he would ask his customers if they knew anyone else who was interested in buying a car, and often they would. One night, Halle met with a couple at 7:00 p.m., sold them a car and, via their referrals, sold two more cars to their neighbors by midnight the same night. That type of success was addictive to a struggling father and college student, and Halle was determined to get more of it.

Halle and Adams received 20 percent of the first $200 profit the dealership made and then 50 percent of the next $300 of profit, which encouraged the college students to upsell more aggressively.

"When I was talking to people and they were interested in a car, I'd say to them, 'Now this is the car we talked about and it's going to cost you $67 a month. You can afford that. But maybe you want to add something to it or go to a little bit better model. For $75 a month, for $7 more, you could have this.' People would say that would be kind of cool. Well, you took $7 times thirty-six months and that's a lot of money. And I got half of it. So, I was making a lot of money," Halle remembers.

Halle earned $11,600 selling cars in 1956, the year he graduated from Michigan Normal. At the time, the price of a new home was approximately $11,700 and the average U.S. worker was earning less than $4,500.

As car sales paid off, Bruce and Gerry gained financial security. Gerry had been keeping the family finances in line, much as Bruce's mother had done, as he relied on a GI Bill benefit of about $110 per month and wages at the Ford plant. Now, as sales commissions multiplied the family's earnings, Gerry socked away the extra dollars for a down payment on a home.

"We were young people from working class families in Detroit," Halle says. "Neither one of us had any money. When I got out of the Marine Corps, we had between $700 and $800. That's what we had. Two years later, in the fall, I put $5,000 down and bought a house in Belleville, Michigan. So, we bought a new house after two years and we're still in college." Still, Halle wasn't satisfied with selling cars. The pay was good, even great, but he didn't see a lifetime career for himself as a car salesman. When he graduated in the spring of 1956, Halle sought a career path more fitting for a man of his new stature. One night, at a drive-in movie theater with Gerry and Bruce Jr., Halle went to the snack bar at intermission and ran into an old college friend.

Halle had met Earl Burt when he enrolled at Michigan Normal the first time around. Burt was several years his senior and a very successful person—one of the polished, elegant people who held a mystique for the working-class Halle. Burt was building a career as a life insurance salesman for Connecticut General Life Insurance Company, and Connecticut General was looking for bright young men like Halle. Burt encouraged him to sign up for the management-training program, and Halle thought he had found his path to success.

Connecticut General—which later morphed into CIGNA—provided a starting salary of $7,000, which was roughly 60 percent of the income Halle was bringing home from car sales, but much more than the $3,000 to $5,000 salaries offered elsewhere to new business grads. Halle learned the ropes and returned to Michigan so confident of success that he and Gerry sold their first home and bought a new place in Dearborn Heights.

"I thought that the education that I got at Connecticut General was probably more effective—a better, more direct education—than what I received in college," Halle says. "It was practical, business oriented, down to earth. It was wonderful. I've been grateful to Connecticut General for years for that."

The beauty of insurance sales, of course, is the stream of annual commissions that come from renewals. Over time, a successful agent can earn a substantial income simply by keeping clients happy. As he returned home and tried to create that stream for himself, though, Halle discovered a major difference between selling cars—or tires—and selling insurance.

"In the tire business, I'm in a store and they come in the store. Why? Because they want tires. I'm not going to their house and trying to sell tires. Why am I at their house? I'm trying to tell them they need life insurance, which they probably don't. Or they don't want to buy or they don't want to allocate the funds," he says.

Halle followed the usual pattern for new life insurance salesmen, calling on friends, relatives and anyone else he met over the ensuing two years. As his family started to grow—Susan was born on Halle's twenty-seventh birthday, May 27, 1957, and Lisa would follow on November 29, 1958—the insurance business and Bruce Halle proved to be a mismatch.

Halle began preparing income tax returns as a sideline to his insurance business, which kept him in contact with many of his old friends and colleagues. One such contact was Harry Regetz, who had offered Bruce his first job as a car salesman. Another was Bill DiDonato, whose wedding was the locale for Bruce's prediction that he would marry Geraldine Konfara.

Bill DiDonato graduated two years before Bruce and the two had not seen each other since DiDonato's wedding. When they reconnected, Halle's old friend was the proud new owner of Automotive Supply Company, which sold tires and various car parts to gas stations and car dealers. Bill was struggling and Bruce, a business genius and insurance dud, thought he had the smarts to turn Bill's business around.

Halle and DiDonato agreed that Halle would join Automotive Supply, but not as an employee. Halle wanted to be an owner in the worst way—which turned out to be exactly how he did it.

The two agreed that Halle would buy 25 percent of Automotive Supply for $5,000, and the two would run the company together. Of course, Halle had put all his savings into a home two years earlier and had barely covered his expenses during his failed insurance career. He and Gerry had no money to invest, so Halle paid a visit to Harry Regetz, who agreed to lend him the $5,000 to buy into DiDonato's business. Again, Halle had found someone willing to place a bet on his ability and determination to perform.

Bruce had the determination, but the challenges of the business were more than he and Bill could manage. Bill had bought Automotive Supply Company from Gallup-Silkworth Company, an oil and gasoline distributor. Because auto parts were just a sideline, Gallup-Silkworth could make a profit from the business. As an independent company, however, Automotive Supply was not sustainable.

"The biggest problem we had was accounts receivable," Halle remembers. "Bill was a sweetheart guy. He trusted everybody. He trusted your worst enemy and gave them credit. He was just that way, and when I joined him, one of my first goals was to collect all the accounts receivable that Bill had that were past due and not being paid. So, I worked hard, and we got that to where we had at least enough cash to stay alive."

Harry Regetz pitched in to help, teaching Bruce some lessons along the way. Harry was an old German man, very conservative with his cash. He had lent Bruce $5,000 on Bruce's promise to repay $100 a month until the debt was covered. When Harry lent Bruce his stake in the company, Harry was retired and a bit bored. He asked if he could help out with sales.

"In Manchester, Michigan, about twenty or thirty miles away, there was a large German Mason community and I used to go up there and call on the car dealers and gas stations and practically sell them nothing," Halle remembers. "Harry was German and he was a Mason and had a Mason ring. He'd go out there and he'd come back with $2,000 worth of sales every time."

Regetz's support was not sufficient to keep the wholesale business afloat, so Halle and DiDonato decided to open a retail store as a way to build sales and, potentially, margins. Halle rented an old gas station in Ypsilanti and opened his first retailing venture. Automotive Supply was a Firestone dealer, so the retail store was also expected to offer Firestone tires exclusively.

"In those days, before the laws were changed, you had to be pure," Halle explains. "You sold Firestone and nothing else. You couldn't have another tire in your building. Well, I wasn't that pure, so when I opened the store and started to get going, I bought some other tires from another distributor, the Isaacson Brothers out of Toledo, Ohio."

The Isaacsons, who owned World Tire, would later become a driving force in Bruce Halle's success, but the decision to augment his Firestone offerings with Uniroyal tires from the Isaacsons spelled disaster for Bruce and Bill. When Firestone learned that Halle was selling another company's tires, they pulled their franchise, product and even the sign on the store.

As 1959 drew to a close, Bruce and Bill decided to call it quits. They divided up their resources and debts and closed the business, but remained friends. In the three years since Bruce Halle had graduated from Michigan Normal, his fortunes had moved strongly in reverse. In 1956, he earned $11,600 and was living in his own house. In 1959, he had no job, no prospects and approximately $17,000 in debts—excluding his mortgage of roughly $15,000.

With a wife and three children to support, Halle began casting about for ideas. Bob McShane, an upperclassman when Halle enrolled at Holy

Redeemer and now a commercial insurance salesman, had reconnected with Halle and DiDonato during the previous year. McShane began insuring Automotive Supply and often ate lunch with its owners as they sought to build and, later, close the company.

Bruce came up with three ideas in the fall of 1959, McShane remembers: selling factory-second shoes, hawking day-old bread and opening a retail tire store. McShane couldn't see any of those options as a path to success, but he was particularly doubtful about Halle continuing in the same business that he'd just closed.

"I said, 'Everybody sells tires. I don't think that's a good idea, Bruce,'" McShane remembers. As it turns out, he was wrong.

SIX TIRES, NO PLAN

Christmas 1959 was not the most joyous holiday that Bruce and Gerry Halle would share. For Bruce Jr., age seven, Susan, age two, and Lisa, just one year old, the decorations on the tree and the treats that Gerry baked would make for a festive season. However, just as Bruce had no sense of his parents' financial challenges in Berlin, the children would not realize that their own world had crumbled.

Bruce and Gerry had ridden a roller coaster during the eight years of their marriage—from separation during the Korean War to the scrimping during Bruce's college years; from the successful salesmanship skills that provided a down payment on a new home to his failed career moves into insurance and auto parts. Now, as the year came to a close, Bruce was planning yet another venture: a tire store.

As Bill DiDonato and Bruce Halle split up their business, each took on his share of debts and assets. Bill kept the store in Ypsilanti, which he later renamed Spartan Tire, while Bruce held onto two new tires, six recaps (retreads) and a wooden box filled with assorted gas caps, filters and other detritus of a failed distribution business.

Despite the odds, Bruce thought he might have a few advantages as a tire retailer. The retail store he operated while in partnership with DiDonato had been profitable, unlike the distribution business itself. While he wasn't all that good at selling insurance, Halle had proved to be quite capable of selling physical goods, including both cars and tires. After working his way through school, he'd learned how to put in the hours needed to make a retail store successful.

Halle had one more thing going for him as he considered his future. He had no choice. "Tires were the first adventure when I was stuck," he admits. "I had to open the tire store to work my way out of that mess."

Uniroyal gave Halle a year to pay the $12,000 he owed the company. Ten years later, Halle would ask the credit manager, Andrew Stone, why Uniroyal was willing to believe in him and give him more time to pay. "Bruce," Stone answered, "you didn't have anything we could take, anyway."

Halle rented an old plumbing supply building at 2266 West Stadium Boulevard in Ann Arbor, in the shadow of a Goodyear tire store. He cleaned out the building, built countertops, painted a sign, put his six tires proudly on display and opened in January, 1960. It took three days before his first customer came in, and it was another four days before he sold his first tire.

Halle chose the name Discount Tire to tell customers they could get a good deal at his store. Fair-trade laws allowed manufacturers to lock in the retail price of their products, but off-brand discounters were emerging as an increasingly common source of goods.

Years later, business school students and Discount Tire employees would ask Halle about the insightful strategy and brilliant business plan he had developed as he prepared to open his first store. His answer is always the same: there was no plan.

"I was married. We had three children then. I didn't have a job and I had to make a living, pay the rent, buy the bread and milk and the groceries and maybe a pair of shoes," he says. "That was the business plan: go into the store and sell as many tires as I can each day and hopefully be able to pay for those things."

Rent at the first store was $400 per month and electric costs were low, especially since Bruce had no compressor or other machinery. He had an air tank that would hold up to sixty pounds of air, but the pressure in the tank and the tire was equalized after he filled a single tire to thirty pounds per square inch. Each tire would require a separate trip across the street to the Zephyr gas station, where Halle could fill his air tank at no cost.

If Bruce could sell seven or eight tires per day, he could cover the rent, pay the mortgage, buy groceries for the family and stay afloat. At the time, a tire might sell for $7 to $9, with a profit of just $1 to $2, but most replacement tires required tubes, and the tubes had a much higher markup. An average inner tube cost about a dollar but sold for roughly three times that much.

Chastened by his failures of the prior three years, Bruce asked Gerry to start up a fund and build a cushion of $1,500 to carry them over when—not if—the business failed. After the $1,500 was saved, Gerry could use any excess money for drapes or clothing or whatever the growing family might need.

Halle benefited from an asset that Thomas Stanley and William Danko would write about years later in *The Millionaire Next Door:* a wife who was great on defense. "Gerry was very conservative with money. It wasn't like I was married to a wife that wanted this and wanted that and so on and so forth and could get us into financial disaster. We didn't have that," Halle says with a sense of gratitude that continues to this day.

"During the early days in the company, we weren't going out much at night," Halle says. "Once in a while, like maybe on a Saturday night or Sunday night, Gerry and I might go out for a little dinner. Our social life was pretty minimal. Just our friends, a few neighbors and her mother and father, who were alive then, and my mom and dad were, too."

Clipping coupons and relishing the opportunity to get a bargain became a lifelong pattern for Gerry, even as the company's fortunes eliminated any requirements for that kind of thrift. Saving a few dollars would continue to give her a sense of pride even when it would be far from necessary. In the early 1980s, coming home on the company plane, Gerry would regale Diane Fournier, wife of now-COO Steve Fournier, with stories of coupons she had found and money she had saved. She would see no contradiction between saving on groceries and flying on a private jet.

Reflecting his religious tradition, Bruce decided to close his store on Sunday and from noon until 3:00 p.m. on Good Friday—both policies that remain in full effect today. Although retailers were increasingly adopting Sunday hours as suburbia spread and shopping centers multiplied, Halle made the personal decision to be with his family one day each week. After he stopped working in the stores, he would maintain that policy for all the employees who followed.

Just as Bruce's father had spent much of his time away from family, working multiple jobs, Bruce was matching that pattern at his infant company. The fledgling entrepreneur was out the door early each morning to clean and open the store and wait for customers to arrive. In the evening, he'd drive to other tire dealers and wholesalers to replenish his supply of whatever tires or tubes he'd happened to sell that day.

Most days were slow, however, and Bruce spent a good deal of his time playing euchre with seventy-year-old Fred Lirette, a polished and elegant former Ford executive who had worked with Halle and DiDonato. "I got him in the divorce," Halle would joke, but Lirette was a valuable asset. Sociable and smart, he could answer the phone or entertain customers while Bruce was out in the cold, changing tires. A customer might appreciate the deal he got on a set of tires, but customers didn't know one tire from another. What they did recognize was courtesy, friendliness and a clean store, all of which would become touchstones of the company.

The sign on the building said Discount Tire and Halle was a discounter from day one. His product line consisted almost entirely of off-brand tires, generally made by subsidiaries of brand-name manufacturers like Goodyear, Uniroyal and BF Goodrich. Often, Halle's tires would have the same tread signature as the name brands and he would promote them as made by the same manufacturer.

His location next to a Goodyear store proved to be an advantage as customers noticed his sign and ventured over to check him out. Many of the major-brand retailers would sneer when a customer asked about

Discount Tire, which had the unintended effect of making them more curious about the store.

Still, Halle needed a good gimmick to build his customer counts. As spring arrived, he offered to change snow tires at no cost. Snow tires were very common in northern states like Michigan, where motorists went through two cycles—one on and one off—each year. Drivers who came in to change their tires for free might be enticed to return when they needed new tires later.

The tire-changing service proved to be a winner for Discount Tire, with customers lining up around the block at times to take advantage of the deal. Customers who received the free service would send their friends, and many would come back for new tires. The word-of-mouth benefits proved substantial. The Stadium Boulevard store was profitable in its first year, and Gerry had saved up her $1,500 emergency fund. At that point, Halle and Lirette were the only employees, and the retired Ford manager was more interested in having something to do than in earning a paycheck.

As 1960 progressed, Halle began to see the patterns of the business. The streets would be empty when the University of Michigan was playing in a football game, which gave him plenty of time to play euchre with Lirette. Customers usually knew little about tires and tended to feel most comfortable with the same brand that had come with their cars. In Halle's case, that often created the need to explain that his tires were made by the same manufacturer that made the tires on their car, but he was offering them at a better price.

As customer counts increased and the company became more profitable, Halle bought a used air compressor, which freed him from his ordeal of one trip to the gas station for each tire he sold. The compressor increased his productivity dramatically—Halle was doing all the manual labor while Fred served primarily as euchre tutor and kibitzer-in-chief.

Halle benefited from both his physical stamina and his refusal to be defeated a third time. Each evening, after closing the store, Halle would drive to various suppliers for tires, tubes and other supplies before heading home with his bag of cash, checks and paperwork from the day just ended. The accounting office was at the kitchen table, where he tallied the day's receipts and prepared his deposit slip for the next morning's visit to his bank.

Halle, his clothes, even the money carried the smells of the tire store into the home, and Halle's daughters began to associate that aroma with success—much the same way the residents of Berlin had taken a perverse pride in the scent of the paper mills. Years later, when Susan, Lisa and Gerry would pass through the tire section in their local Costco, they'd laugh and say it "smells like money."

Halle agrees that the smell of the store would "clear your nostrils out" each morning. Bringing home the bag of cash at night was one of the highlights of his first years in business.

"I'd come home and I'd be very excited, you know? I had a great day and I'd dump it on the table and Gerry and I would count it out. It was amazing. 'Look what I did today! Look at all this money!' It was fun and it was kind of a cool thing," Halle remembers.

Halle's daughters remember that their father's hands were continuously bandaged from the cuts and scrapes that came with changing tires. "He'd do the dishes at night because that was the only way his hands would always get cleaned," remembers daughter Susan Lyle.

Deeply in debt, Halle's financial position was precarious at best during the company's first years. While the business became profitable very quickly on an operating basis, Halle was continually strapped for cash to buy more inventory and pay down his debts to Uniroyal and Harry Regetz. Discount Tire was at risk of collapse from almost any type of effective competition during its earliest stages. The nearby Goodyear store, gas stations and other competitors had deeper pockets or additional product lines to protect them if they decided to match or undercut Halle's prices. None considered the tiny store on Stadium Boulevard to be a threat, however—certainly not enough of a threat for them to cut their own prices in response. Protected by competitors' inertia, Halle had the opportunity to grow.

By 1961, just a year after opening, Discount Tire was on a roll. Word of mouth was drawing an increasing number of customers, and revenue grew rapidly. Growth presented cash flow issues, however, as Halle still

SIX TIRES, NO PLAN

lacked the capital to buy tires in volume or the credit lines to buy now and pay later. His credit problems were resolved, however, by two brothers from Toledo, Ohio—Maury and Jay Isaacson.

The Isaacson brothers owned a tire distribution business called World Tire, and they had sold tires to Halle when he was running the retail store he owned with Bill DiDonato. Looking to expand, they decided to reconnect with Halle and drove up to Ann Arbor, just forty miles away. The Isaacsons told Halle he could order up to forty tires at a time, on credit, with sixty days to pay. There would be no contract—the Isaacsons would trust Halle to do the right thing and pay his bills. As Sister Marie Ellen, Ray Walk and Harry Regetz had done before them, the Isaacsons saw something in Bruce that they liked and trusted. He was determined to earn that trust.

The boost from the Isaacsons helped Halle keep more tires in stock and reduced the amount of time he spent each day picking up tires from various suppliers. While the relationship with Halle proved highly profitable for World Tire, Halle's relationship with the Isaacsons became a catalyst for Discount Tire's growth. The store posted revenues of $110,000 in 1962—the equivalent of selling full sets of tires and tubes for roughly six cars per day—and Halle's gross profit was 23 percent.

Halle changed the tires, kept the books and cleaned the toilets on Stadium Boulevard. Even though sales were growing, Halle was hesitant about adding full-time employees to the start-up business. He had returned to the income levels of his car-selling days, but he was more cautious than he might have been in earlier years. As sales grew in 1962, though, he was confident enough to begin hiring part-time workers during heavy periods.

As winter came to Michigan that year, Halle recruited Gerry's first cousin, a fifteen-year-old high school student named Gary Van Brunt, as one of his first part-time workers. Van Brunt's father, John, had obtained the funding for the Halle's wedding from his boss, Raymond Walk. John Van Brunt died a few years later, when Gary was nine years old, and Bruce and Gerry became an increasingly close part of his extended family. At thirty-two years old, Bruce was a role model for the fatherless teen.

"One day, Bruce called the house and said, 'What are you doing Saturday?'" Van Brunt relates. "I said, 'I'm waiting for it to snow so I can shovel some sidewalks and make a few bucks.' He said, 'Yeah, me too, I'm waiting for it to snow. I've got lots of snow tires and I need some help at the store. You're kind of mechanical and you've worked on cars, so how would you like to come to work on Saturday?' I'd never changed a tire out of a wheel, but he said, 'We'll show you how to do that.' So, he picked me up and we stopped at a couple places to pick up some tires that people had ordered and we got to the store and there were two college kids there, Jack Bailey and Freddy Sanchez. They showed me how to jack up a car and take the assembly off. I'd take it inside, they would change the tire and balance it and I'd take it out and put it back on."

Halle paid Van Brunt $10 per day for ten hours of work. After a month, he offered the teen a regular part-time job, with a warning. Van Brunt recalls, "He said, 'There's something that we have to get straight. The two worst people in the world to hire are friends and relatives. First off, if you hire a friend and he doesn't work out and you have to fire him, then you've not only lost an employee, but you've lost a friend. The second is a relative. If you hire a relative and he doesn't work out and I have to fire you, then the whole family is impacted, but you're still a relative. That's not good either. So here's how it's going to be. From 8:30 'til 6:00, you're an employee. The rest of the time you're a relative. If we have a problem during the day or something and you're supposed to be at my house for dinner that night, you better be smiling, because then you're a relative.' And that's how we kept it all these years."

Van Brunt had been working part-time jobs since his father died, babysitting for the Halle daughters, shoveling snow and cutting grass. As he earned more money at the store, he bought a car that he used to make pickups before he went to work. The system was simple—he would call the store collect and, if they needed something, Halle would accept the charges. If not, no expenses were incurred. Van Brunt saved costs further by reclaiming broken pieces of chalk—which he used to mark tire inventory—from tire suppliers who were rich enough to toss out a piece of chalk that was only half used.

As the Stadium store became well established, Halle began to consider how he could grow his business further. Goodyear had multiple stores. Firestone had multiple stores. Sears had multiple stores. There was even a tiny hamburger chain, McDonald's, that was opening multiple stores. Why not Discount Tire?

It was something of a leap for a store owner to consider additional outlets while he was still paying off his creditors. Halle was relatively fearless, however, and a bit headstrong. Discount Tire's model was very simple: offer low-priced products, convince customers they were getting a deal, give them surprising benefits like free snow tire mounting or clean bathrooms and try to build positive word of mouth. As that model proved profitable, all Halle needed were the people and money to multiply the footprint.

Halle had been favorably impressed by a tire salesman at a nearby General Tire store, Ted Von Voigtlander, and began talking with him about coming to work with Discount Tire. Halle offered Von Voigtlander the same opportunity DiDonato had given Halle. With an investment of a few thousand dollars to help finance a second store, Von Voigtlander would be a 49 percent partner in the company. In 1963, Bruce Halle and his new partner prepared to open their second store.

'TIL DEATH DO US PART

To a large extent, the still-fledgling Discount Tire Company was already driven by personality as much as product. Halle was selling off-brand tires and giving away free services, which limited margins. The only way to make much profit was by pumping up sales volume and that, in turn, required word of mouth from happy customers. The person selling and installing the tires—usually Halle himself—would have to use his customer contact time to build rapport and entice follow-up sales.

When Von Voigtlander joined the company, he mirrored Halle's willingness to work hard and smile while doing it. He encouraged customers to remember the company, to appreciate the deal they were getting and to recommend Discount Tire to their friends. As a team, the two partners began to work as one.

Halle and Von Voigtlander rented an old gas station building in Ypsilanti, across town from the tire shop Bill DiDonato was operating, and opened their second store in 1964. Michigan offered a tax exemption for the first $25,000 of income per corporation during this time, so the partners took advantage of the break by incorporating the facility separately as Tire Wonderland. Von Voigtlander brought in a friend, Mickey Smith, to manage the store as he and Halle continued working at the Stadium Boulevard store and considered further growth opportunities.

In the 1960s, summer weekends with family were almost as hectic as working. Bruce would close the store on Saturday afternoon, pick up Gerry and the children and get on the road for a five-hour drive to a campground on Lake Michigan. Much as his own family had ventured to Dolly Copp from Berlin, the Halles would spend Saturday night and Sunday camping before driving home late in the day on packed two-lane roads. On Monday mornings, Bruce would leave home at 6:30, picking up tires along the way to his store in Ann Arbor.

Even in the busiest times, the Halle children saw their lives as normal, much as Bruce viewed his own childhood in Berlin. Bruce helped his children with homework, Gerry kept the house running, and the couple caught up on the details of the day when Bruce came home at night. Halle's children remember the pair as particularly affectionate, holding hands and calling each other pet names on a daily basis.

With a partner and a second store, Halle became increasingly optimistic and, to a great degree, fearless about money. In 1964, the same year he and Von Voigtlander opened the second store, Bruce and Gerry traded up to a newer, more expensive home in Ann Arbor, closer to the Stadium Boulevard store. Halle persuaded the developer to sell him the property and build the house with almost no down payment—and then scavenged rocks and rubble from a nearby highway construction site to build a wall along the driveway with Bruce Jr. The house had an outdoor swimming pool, which immediately raised the social status of the Halle children.

While Bruce Jr. carried on the tradition of his father and grandfather by joining the football team at St. Thomas High School, Susan and Lisa began riding horses at a nearby stable. Halle bought Susan her first horse, a seventeen-hand thoroughbred named Highpockets.

In 1965, Bruce bought a working farm at Boyne Mountain that became the family's weekend retreat. In the summer, the family would spend time outdoors at the Boyne Mountain farmhouse and, in the winter, they'd go skiing in the same area. By the end of the decade, they would up their game by venturing out to Aspen, Colorado, for their first ski trip out west. In the same period, Bruce would buy Gerry her first mink stole, making her the first woman on her block with a fashionable fur.

Bruce and Gerry spent their free time together or with a small group of close friends and family. Increasingly, that group included the employees who were pinning their career hopes on the budding entrepreneur. On Sundays, when the stores were closed, the Halles would often host barbecues or other gatherings for employees and their families, creating connections that tied employees more closely to each other, to the company and to Halle. Gerry relished the role of Discount Tire Mom and worked to make sure both husbands and wives felt like part of the family.

From the start, Halle wanted his employees to be very happy. While he cannot recall a time when he analyzed the connection between happy employees and good customer service, Halle recognized the strong link between the two. Customers who are treated rudely don't return. Employees who are miserable at work are less likely to treat their customers well. Therefore, he couldn't keep customers happy unless he made his employees happy first.

When the stores were busy, Halle expected full commitment from his workers to get customers serviced quickly and with a smile. During slower times, the men at the Stadium Boulevard store would play touch football with Jack Carpenter's employees at Perfect Fit Seat Covers, which shared a parking lot with the store.

"Jack Carpenter made seat covers and convertible tops, primarily for boats," Gary Van Brunt recalls. "We shared a common driveway, and when it snowed, Jack would be out there in the morning plowing. In the wintertime, his business would fall off and our business would increase, so he was there to help us if a car got stuck, to push cars in. When the air hoses would freeze up, we'd take them over to Jack's place and he would shoot steam through them to thaw them and then blow air through the hoses to dry them out. When there was a football game going on, business would go to nothing, so we'd play football in the parking lot with his team and our team. When we'd rip our pants squatting down and so forth, we'd take them over there and they had sewing machines and he'd sew up our pants. We had a lot of fun with Jack."

In turn, Jack Carpenter had his fun with the men of Discount Tire. When his neighbors brought pants in for repair, the results were often unexpected. At times, he would sew the pant legs shut or stitch the employee's wallet into the back pocket. "You'd go for lunch and reach for your wallet and you couldn't get it out," Van Brunt remembers.

Fun was a critical ingredient for Halle from day one with Fred Lirette. If the workplace was fun, people would feel more like teammates, and teammates worked harder to make the entire team successful. The fun quotient increased in the mid-1960s when Fred Halle retired from Ford Motor Company and began helping out at the Stadium Boulevard store. Still vital and a hard worker—he would live to be ninety-two years old—Fred Halle was back on stage, even if the audience consisted of a bunch of tire changers and the crew at Perfect Fit Seat Covers. The first store also became a magnet for Bruce Halle Jr., now a teen doing odd jobs around the store in much the same way that Gary Van Brunt had done a few years earlier.

Halle and Von Voigtlander had depended on word of mouth and some traditional print advertising to build brand awareness for the first two stores, but they upped the ante in 1966 with eye-catchingly weird ads in a start-up paper called the *Huron Valley Ad-Visor*.

"Wayne Alber was the guy who was starting it up, and Wayne was a creative guy," Halle remembers. Ted and Bruce dressed up as Batman and Robin, as aliens in a flying saucer, as the Cartwrights from the television show *Bonanza*—pretty much anything to get a laugh or a second look. "People would see these ads and wonder, 'Who are these crazy guys? Let's go see them!' We gave away geraniums, watermelons—anything for some goodwill. In town, there was a Goodyear and a Firestone tire store and a General Tire store. They were just staid old places and they didn't do anything. We're doing this off-the-wall stuff."

Halle and Von Voigtlander opened their third store, in Flint, Michigan, in 1966 and followed quickly with a fourth store, the second in Ann Arbor, in 1967 and one in Kalamazoo in 1968. They built their team by reconnecting with friends and relatives, former classmates and business contacts.

Dave Fairbanks, who had met Bruce as a freshman at Michigan State Normal College and helped him move his massive inventory of six tires into the first store, joined Halle in 1966 after working his way up to principal at Willow Run High School in Ypsilanti. Fairbanks had watched his friend building a business and thought the growing company—and its founder—offered more career potential than the school.

"When I was a principal, I had to hire teachers at $5,500 per year, and here Bruce was, hiring people to come in and change tires for $7,700 per year," Fairbanks remembers. New stores would need new managers, and Fairbanks, whose grandparents owned a grocery store when he was young, thought it would be great to manage his own store. While he was earning much more as a high school principal than he would as a tire changer, he saw more upside over the long term from building a business. Beyond the opportunity for higher income as a store manager, Fairbanks liked the idea of working with his old friend.

As Halle considered further expansion of the company, however, he began to realize that he had put himself into a box. He could not add more partners and still be the majority owner of the company.

When the entire staff consisted of a few part-timers and one Marine sergeant, Discount Tire operated on the "cigar box" accounting system. Whatever money was left in the cigar box at the end of the day was Halle's to keep. Not much of that accounting system changed when Ted Von Voigtlander came on as his partner.

What had changed was Halle's willingness to give up ownership in the company. He hadn't thought much about a third or fourth or fifth store when he courted Von Voigtlander to help him finance store number two. He acted rashly, though, in giving up 49 percent ownership in return for the single infusion of cash for the second store. Once his share had dropped to 51 percent, Halle had no more equity to cede. If he wanted to attract the right people to run future stores, he would need some other approach to compensation.

When Fairbanks joined the company, he wanted to come in as a part-owner, as Von Voigtlander had done. Halle didn't want to drop his ownership level below the 51 percent he'd agreed to with Von Voigtlander, so he made a deal with the two men. Fairbanks would invest $10,000 to own 30 percent of the company's fourth store—which opened in 1967 in an old Lincoln-Mercury dealership in Ann Arbor—and Bruce would adjust his compensation to give Ted a bigger cut of the rest of the profits. Nearly forty-five years later, Fairbanks still owns 30 percent of that store, making him the only person other than Bruce Halle to have any equity investment in a Discount Tire store.

Fairbanks's store opened as Huron Valley Tire and marked the first—and only—time the company would offer general repairs, alignment and other services in a Discount Tire store. Many major tire dealers and most gas stations offered mechanical work, so the added source of revenue seemed like a natural fit.

It wasn't. Changing tires was a high-volume, quick-turnover business. Margins were lower than for general car maintenance, but the store could make up the difference in volume. Better yet, tire changers earned far less per hour than mechanics. As Fairbanks, Halle and Von Voigtlander learned to their dismay, mechanics looked down on the grunt work performed by tire jockeys, so they would resist helping when they were idle and the tire changers were overworked.

"Uniroyal gave us projections about how much service work could be done in a store that also sold tires," Fairbanks remembers. "Over a period of time, we found that the newer cars did not need the alignments, brakes and mufflers replaced as often as the old cars used to. We also found that the alignments they projected could never be done in the time they said they should be done."

Meanwhile, Uniroyal's reputation as a tire brand was not particularly strong, and it became harder to sell tires as a Uniroyal dealer. Halle and Fairbanks met with a rep from the tire company, and Halle asked Fairbanks if he wanted to continue as a Uniroyal dealer. Fairbanks said "no" and Halle dropped Uniroyal on the spot, winning added loyalty from his former classmate and moving the product/service mix into sync with the company's three other stores.

Two years after Dave Fairbanks cast his lot with Halle, Al Olsen, a deputy sheriff in Washtenaw County, was looking for a new line of work. Olsen and Fairbanks would soon be instrumental in building the company, but in the mid-1960s, they were merely two young guys looking for an opportunity to grow.

Olsen had worked in retail at a Food Fair grocery store when he was in high school, and he liked the environment. Better yet, his boss liked him and gave him added responsibility. When Olsen graduated from high school, he went to work full time at the store and became an assistant manager.

In 1959, Olsen joined the Army and became a military police officer. When he left in 1962, he drifted into civilian police work and was earning about $15,000 a year, plus benefits, as a sheriff's deputy in 1967. As civil unrest increased during the Vietnam War and the Civil Rights Movement, police work in a college campus community lost much of its charm.

Olsen was a friend of Mickey Smith, who managed the Ypsilanti store, and Olsen had been one of Smith's first customers. "Mickey always told me, 'Someday you're going to get tired of police work. You should talk to Bruce when you're ready,'" Olsen remembers.

In April 1968, Olsen pulled up in his squad car for a twenty-minute interview with Ted and Bruce in Ann Arbor. At the end of the interview, Ted said Olsen would hear from them in a week, but by the time Olsen reached home, Ted had already called. Olsen gave his notice and began working at the Stadium store two weeks later. He loved the company immediately.

"The culture of the company is very, very simple," remarked Olsen. "Bruce said, 'Respect your fellow employees. Look after each other. Take your customers in as family.' How are you going to treat your customers if you, in your mind, say, 'That's my dad coming in?' That was laid out to me in the first three days, and it's comforting."

After just three days at the Stadium store, Ted announced that he and Bruce had taught Al everything they could about the company and sent him to work under Smith at the Ypsilanti store. Within three years, he was a store manager making as much as he had made as a deputy sheriff and he exceeded that level substantially in subsequent years.

Al and his wife, Judy, had done a bit of soul-searching before Olsen took the job at half the salary and with none of the benefits he had been accustomed to as a deputy sheriff. Judy agreed to go to work as a way of reducing their economic burden—a significant step in the mid-1960s. After his family and other contacts learned he was going to work in a tire store, he began receiving competing job offers—including one from his father.

Olsen called Halle for a follow-up discussion, and Halle invited the Olsens to his home the following Sunday. After dinner, Gerry and Judy developed their own friendship while Al and Bruce discussed plans for the company. Halle said he hoped to have twelve stores within three years, and that Olsen would be one of the managers.

"I told Bruce that night, ''til death do us part. I will not be lured away.' I just needed the comfort and understanding that he intended to grow and I was going to be part of it," Olsen said.

As Halle and Von Voigtlander opened new stores and recruited the men to manage them, employee motivation and rewards became a relevant topic. After taking Von Voigtlander in as a partner and then making a special deal with Fairbanks, Halle had given up all the equity he was willing to cede. He would have to find another way to attract and retain good people.

Halle didn't want his people working on commission. He knew from his own experience that commissions created the temptation for extra upselling. Upselling had worked for him as a car salesman, when he convinced buyers they could afford an extra payment of $3 or $7 or $10 per month. At Discount Tire, however, the most powerful calling card was savings. If customers had the sense they were being lured in by cheap prices, only to be pressured by commission salesmen, the company would suffer. Bait-and-switch marketing would not drive referrals or repeat business.

As with most decisions, Halle was more intuitive than analytical. He wanted to attract good people with good personalities, integrity and a solid work ethic. And he would have to pay them well enough to retain them.

"I wanted all my full-time people to make $10,000 a year," Halle says, recalling a nice, round number that he had pulled out of the ether. "I just picked $10,000. That was big money. People who graduated college didn't make that much money. And, we're a little tire store and you can make $10,000. That's kind of cool! It was cool, and it helped me get good people and keep good people."

Halle began implementing his grand strategy as the company started to expand in the mid-1960s. Although he didn't have the cash flow to bring people in at the $10,000 level, he sought to bring people up to that level as they proved themselves in the stores.

As the advertising and word of mouth spread and stores multiplied, revenues multiplied as well. By 1969, sales reached $1.7 million. Tubeless tires had become the norm for new cars late in the 1950s and the replacement market followed several years later, making tubes a much smaller component of the total than they had been when Halle opened the first store in 1960. In the meantime, the company more than compensated with higher customer counts.

Upheaval in the tire industry provided significant benefits for Discount Tire. Overall, quality control was poor and the original equipment tires on American cars were often undersized—possibly to save money—relative to the weight they were carrying.

Discount Tire continued to sell off brands, usually made by the big-name manufacturers. Peerless tires came from Uniroyal, Lee was part of Goodyear, Carnegie was made for the Isaacson brothers by Firestone. The Isaacson brothers at World Tire continued to be Discount Tire's biggest suppliers, but Halle, Von Voigtlander and Van Brunt started looking for additional sources for product. Even with multiple stores in the late 1960s, the company was far too small to deal directly with most manufacturers. For customers, though, the off brands were usually a better deal.

"The only difference might be in the tread design," says Dave Fairbanks. "When you had the tire with all the plies in there, you could basically have the same tire." Often, tire companies would manage their inventory by unloading blemished tires on second-tier dealers like Discount Tire. "You could have some kind of blemish on the whitewalls, but it was the same tire," Fairbanks recalls. In fact, he adds, the tire companies would sometimes mark tires as "blems" simply to reduce inventories, even if the tires had no blemishes or other flaws.

During this period, it was relatively simple to show that an off-brand replacement tire was superior to the name-brand tire that came with the car. "The original equipment tire by Firestone and Goodyear, in those days, was a two-ply tire. It had a soft sidewall, not like the tires you have on your car today. We had four-ply tires. They were a lot firmer," Halle remembers. "I'd show people the soft little two-ply tire and here's a four-ply tire that is much stronger and safer, and I'd sell them private-brand tires—made by Goodyear, made by Firestone and made by Uniroyal."

As 1969 began, Bruce and Ted were mini-moguls atop a five-store empire that qualified them as very successful businessmen. As they considered their options, they began to look at markets outside of Michigan. Population growth was stronger in the South than in the Rust Belt states, and many of their larger competitors had stores across the nation. It was time to expand their horizons.

ARIZONA INVASION

Halle's early decision to change snow tires as a freebie was a hit in Michigan, but it also highlighted one of the challenges of life in the Snowbelt: snow. Halle and Von Voigtlander were still changing tires occasionally at the Stadium Boulevard store—though other workers handled most of the load—as the winter of 1968-69 ripped across the Wolverine State.

Busting tires is a difficult job in any environment, but handling lug nuts and prying frozen tires off cold metal wheels can be particularly challenging in winter. Tire workers, including Halle, suffered cracked and bleeding skin on their hands during the winter months—an occupational hazard for outdoor jobs.

Discount Tire's sixth store, in Flint, Michigan, was the first built to the company's own design—and even that store had bays exposed to the elements. The store, which opened in the fall of 1968, was five thousand square feet, with inside workspace for mounting, repairing and balancing tires and a showroom with products on display. Its four bays, however, were outside under a canopy. In the winter, tire changers would risk frostbite as they set cars on racks, loosened lug nuts and hoisted wheels from axles. Often, blowing snow would cover the ground under the canopies, forcing workers to shovel their bays before serving the next customer.

As the company began to grow, Halle and Von Voigtlander worked less in the tire shop and spent more time managing the business. Halle was fulfilling a promise he'd made to Dave Fairbanks, Al Olsen and others by creating the opportunity for advancement. Each new store became a reward for the new manager and an enticement for the next man in line: *One day, we'll build a store for you, as well.*

The big question, though, was where to build the next store. Michigan was a big state, and a company with five stores could grow for many years there without saturating its market or cannibalizing its own shops. At the same time, the Sunbelt states offered substantial promise. Rising populations meant more than simply increased demand for replacement tires. New residents to any state might have no particular loyalty to more-established retailers, which could create an opening for an upstart like Discount Tire.

Halle and Von Voigtlander debated the relative merits of Florida, Arizona, Texas and California, ultimately deciding to conduct some field research in Arizona. Halle had been to the state once before—a refueling stop in Prescott on his flight to Camp Pendleton in 1952—but neither partner had any real insight into the area.

What they did have was an appreciation for sunlight. When they got off the plane in April of 1969, the contrast between the climate they'd left and the one they were experiencing was nearly shocking. Both Halle and Von Voigtlander began to reconsider the character-building advantages of winter in Michigan, and each expressed a willingness to make the painful sacrifice of establishing a beachhead in a state without snow.

Halle, with 51 percent of the company, opted to make the move, assuming Gerry was willing. If she wouldn't move to Arizona, Von Voigtlander could do it. Bruce and Gerry flew out in June and made the decision to resettle—they bought their first home during their brief visit and moved to Paradise Valley a few months later.

"You do get a little lucky sometimes," Halle says today. "When I moved to Arizona and started opening stores, as opposed to Michigan, the seasons were an asset to me. When the storms and snow came to the Midwest and it was boomtown out there, it was big-time stuff. And in the spring when they'd take the snow tires off, it was boomtown. In Arizona, it was just more steady, although summers get a little better here. So the mix of climates was a plus. I wasn't smart enough to figure it out at that time, but it was happening and I could see it."

The decades-long population shift into the Sunbelt states has been a major boon for Discount Tire. Today, well over half of the company's stores are south of the Mason-Dixon Line.

"It's not because we were brilliant or smart," Halle says. "We were just lucky. And it's sometimes better to be lucky than smart, because you're never that smart."

Halle scouted sites for the first Arizona store as Von Voigtlander prepared to open the company's sixth and seventh stores in Michigan. Halle's market research involved driving along busy streets and counting both cars and tire stores. The first Arizona store opened on East Thomas Road in January 1970—exactly ten years after Halle had opened his first store in Michigan—and Halle recruited Gerry's cousin, Gary Van Brunt, to move from Ann Arbor to work with him. Van Brunt, now twenty-three, was back only a few days from his honeymoon when Halle asked him to make the move.

"I said, 'Yeah, but now I've got a wife, so I've got to talk to her,'" Van Brunt remembers. "He said, 'Okay, my plane leaves in two hours. Give me a call.' I went home, talked to my wife and called Bruce to say we'd move to Arizona. He said, 'Get some money from Ted and I'll see you next week.' I told him it might take a little longer than that and he said, 'Okay. Two weeks.'"

Van Brunt moved in with the Halles for a month while his wife prepared to transplant their newly formed household from Michigan. Van Brunt worked with Halle at the East Thomas store before they opened Discount Tire's second Arizona store a few months later in Glendale. Just as Halle had done on Stadium Boulevard, Van Brunt built the counters, installed air lines and painted the walls as he prepared to open the Glendale store.

Store growth was organic at Discount Tire. Halle and Von Voigt-lander had no master plan for expansion, but looked for new opportunities as cash allowed. Although the stores were performing well, cash remained scarce, due to the cost of equipment and inventory to equip each location.

"Uniroyal was one of our biggest suppliers, and they were actually in Michigan, so the day that their bill was due, I drove down and got to their front door at 5:00 p.m. Friday so that we had the weekend for some more sales to get cash to cover that," recalls Bob Holman, who joined the company as an accountant in 1969. "That was a regular occurrence, my drive down. Other than that, Bruce was out in Arizona, so I had Arizona checks and Michigan checks and I just used both of them. At that time, there were three or four banks where we could float. That really kept us going for a great deal of time."

Holman, like many others, had joined Discount Tire by chance. Coming home from a job interview, he stopped in at the store on Washtenaw Boulevard to tell his friend, Bob Flavin, that he had been offered a job. The job Holman had been offered wasn't in accounting, but Flavin told him Discount Tire was looking for a new accountant at the time. After a fifteen-minute interview with Von Voigtlander, Holman was starting a thirty-eight-year career with Discount Tire.

"My first office was in the first store and they cleaned out a little wheel room that had used wheels and stuff in it," Holman says. "They took it and painted it and threw a desk in there. That was my first office. Then I started meeting the guys. It was just a fun group of people. I think back then, that was the best part about Discount Tire. Everybody was friends. We did dinner and stuck together for about thirty to forty years after that."

Halle had already moved to Arizona when Holman joined the company, but it was clear from the beginning that he was the senior of the partners.

"Bruce came into town, and he asked what I was getting paid and he said, 'I don't think that's enough.' So, he gave me a raise and, two days later, he left to go back and said, 'I've been thinking about it. That wasn't enough either, so he gave me another raise.' I thought, two raises in two weeks, that's pretty great. I don't think I got another raise for three years, though," Holman recalls.

Holman had doubts about the long-term prospects for the small and undercapitalized company, but his confidence grew as he got to know Halle better.

"I first thought it was a short-term deal, but after meeting and getting to know him, you just knew he was going to succeed," Holman says. "It was the way he treated people. Even back then with the Isaacsons and everything else, everything was a handshake. Those people trusted him, too. There were not a lot of contracts back in those days. So, there's a guy you could shake hands with and it's going to happen. He was really consistent in what he said and it all came true. There were no glitches."

Bruce and Gerry continued the close partnership of their earlier years as they established new patterns in Arizona. One of the girls would fix a scotch and water for Bruce when he came home at night and he and Gerry would discuss the day's events. Daughter Susan recalls the couple blocking out a half hour or an hour to spend time together each night.

Bruce wasn't bringing home a bag of cash from his store each night as had been the case in the early 1960s, but he did bring stories about the challenges and victories of an aspiring tire magnate. Gerry adopted antique shopping as a hobby, scrounging around in little shops to find tire-themed knickknacks to bring home for Bruce. She loved discovering old pieces of Victorian furniture that she could sand, stain and restore.

While Gerry made friends easily in Arizona, she and Bruce were determined to spend their free time with each other. Bruce was either at work or at home and, when he was at home, he was focused on Gerry and the kids.

"The move was great for Mom," says Bruce Halle Jr. "We got landlocked up there in the winter in Michigan, but you can do things here year round. They traveled, they played tennis. It was really good for her."

Although Halle had become more aggressive in his spending while in Michigan—buying a working farm and taking the family on weekend ski trips—the move to Arizona led to greater largesse on many levels. Susan and Lisa had taken up horseback riding in Michigan, and Halle bought horses for both his daughters when they moved to Paradise Valley. Halle bought Bruce Jr. his first motorcycle. Gerry and Bruce bought motorbikes to ride in the desert and joined the Foothills Tennis Club to play tennis with friends.

"We were doing better and so our cost of living was going up a little bit too," Halle remembers. "When I came out here in 1969, I sold the house I had in Ann Arbor to the president of the Ann Arbor Bank for $85,000, and I bought a house out here for $150,000, which was the biggest transaction that the real estate company here had ever had. It was a nice house, two and a half acres in Paradise Alley. It had four bedrooms: two bedrooms upstairs and two down."

The house also had a barn, which enabled Halle to board the girls' horses at home. At the time, families would keep horses at home and ride directly into the desert from their back yards. Often, the girls would ride their horses to a local hamburger stand for lunch. Susan's first horse, Highpockets, remained in Michigan, a gift from Halle to Al and Judy Olsen.

"The girls started showing in little classes around the neighborhood and then they started showing on a bigger level," Halle says. "That really occupied my weekends. I was not working Saturdays anymore, so I'd take the girls, put their horses in the horse trailer and drive to Yuma or Flagstaff or Prescott or Tucson for shows and spend the whole weekend. We'd come back Sunday night late and go to work Monday morning."

While Bruce Jr. focused on football, motorcycles and less-expensive hobbies, horses ratcheted up the family's budget.

"Suddenly, we have horses at the house. Now I've got veterinarians and horseshoers. And we had to go to the shows, so now I've got a trailer and trainers showing the girls how to do the things they did. That started to get expensive, and as I tell people over the years, 'Have boys. They're a lot cheaper. They play football and baseball. It doesn't cost much money.' Horses eat all day long just like you and they get shoes more often than your wife does," Halle laughs.

The girls began to notice that their family's way of life was somewhat more upscale than that of their classmates as Bruce and Gerry took advantage of the opportunity to spoil them. At one point, Gerry suggested to Susan that a debutante ball would be the perfect social soiree for her teenage daughter. Although Susan declined the opportunity, she realized that the family's standing in the community had changed since the move. "Even to this day," Susan says, "I remember my friends saying, 'Can your parents adopt me?'"

While Bruce and Gerry took up tennis and entered a new social circle, Bruce continued to focus almost all his time at work. "Tennis doesn't take much time," he notes, "but golf would have taken the whole weekend and I couldn't do that. My business was taking that time."

Halle never took up golf and declined opportunities to join various business associations or political organizations. Early in his career, he made a commitment to being one of two places: at work or with his family. There were not enough hours in a lifetime to do more, he thought.

As the Halles settled into a new lifestyle in Arizona, the company continued to be primarily an off-brand dealer, and most manufacturers would not deal directly with the still-emerging retailer. Discount Tire relied on the Isaacson brothers' World Tire to supply many of the brand-name products in Michigan and the Isaacsons sought to follow Halle to Arizona, hooking up his business with other distributors they knew.

By that time, however, Halle had his sights on more direct relationships with manufacturers. While he would remain loyal to the Isaacsons long after he was buying almost all his tires directly from manufacturers—reserving a sliver of business for the men who trusted him first—Halle was ready to move up the food chain as a buyer.

He also searched for a new promotional gimmick to surprise customers. He could continue offering free snow tire changes, as he had in Michigan, but he wasn't likely to get many takers in the desert. Halle opted to repair flat tires at no cost, reasoning that this type of pleasant surprise would endear Discount Tire to any customers who happened to walk in with a flat. As in Michigan, the free service was popular with customers but seldom copied by competitors.

Halle continued to feel at home in the stores and would help out by changing tires or unloading inventory when he conducted store visits. His circle of friends, however, began to skew more into the business elite of Arizona. Halle continued to enjoy the rewards of his newfound wealth, investing in a 4,500-acre cattle ranch in Mayer, Arizona. During the same decade, he bought a condominium in a La Jolla, California, development where Motorola chief Robert Galvin, media magnate Karl Eller and real estate investor Russ Lyon also owned apartments. The boy who lived under another family's roof for most of his childhood was now a man of means.

As Halle opened new stores in Arizona and Von Voigtlander spear-headed expansion in Michigan, the company began to develop a farm system for future managers. In 1974, Halle promoted former high-school principal Dave Fairbanks to assistant vice president, with a mandate to oversee Michigan stores and train the next generation of managers.

Halle continued to look eastward to seek talent for his growing base in Arizona, recruiting a second cousin, Steve Fournier, to help build the franchise. Fournier's mother, Charlotte, was Molly Halle's niece and one of the cousins Bruce and his siblings shared holiday dinners with in Berlin. When Charlotte and Roland Fournier took a vacation from Massachusetts to Arizona in 1972, Bruce convinced Charlotte to have Steve interview for a job.

Later that year, Steve Fournier visited Bruce and Gerry in Arizona. Just as he had done with Al Olsen a few years earlier, Halle sat with Fournier at the kitchen table to describe his dreams for the company. Fournier was sold immediately. "If he had sold pogo sticks at the time, I would have gone to work for him," Fournier recalls. Halle was paying $10,000 per year to full-time people, just as he had planned to do shortly after opening his first store ten years earlier. "You go figure, 'I can do that,'" Fournier says.

Fournier interviewed in November, but he wasn't hired to work under Van Brunt in the Glendale store until 1973. Within two years, Van Brunt and Fournier built the Glendale store to the top-grossing outlet in the company. Glendale was the first store to reach $10,000 per day, $100,000 per month and $1,000,000 per year in revenue. Van Brunt would become Discount Tire CEO in 1999 and Fournier would be named chief operating officer the following year.

The next generation of employees also included a second generation of the Halle family, as Bruce Jr. joined Discount Tire as a tire jockey in 1973. Bruce Jr. had started out in the first store at the age of eight, helping with chores as his grandfather had done in the butcher shop in Berlin. He also had resisted joining the family business as a young adult, much as his grandfather had done.

Bruce Jr. worked on the Halle Ranch in Arizona after college, but he was lured back to join his father and cousins at Discount Tire. Like his father, Bruce Jr. started out by busting tires. In 1976, he had earned a position as manager of the company's ninth Arizona store.

As the 1970s progressed, Halle and Von Voigtlander began operating more independently of each other. The partnership remained and Halle continued to own 51 percent of the company, but Von Voigtlander managed Michigan on a day-to-day basis while Halle expanded in Arizona. Increasingly, Halle began moving overall management functions to the Grand Canyon State. In 1974, he moved Bob Holman out from Michigan to manage the financial needs of the company.

"When I moved to Arizona in 1974, Harold Kruder was the accountant in Arizona, and we switched jobs because his parents needed help," Holman remembers. "Harold had just gotten a new house and he asked me to buy his house, but I looked at it and said I couldn't afford it. Then Bruce looked at me and said I could, but I insisted that it was too much money. Then Bruce said, 'I'm the one who's going to pay you. I know you can afford it.' So that was it. I bought the house and, once again, he's going to take care of it."

The corporate presence in Arizona included development of a new advertising strategy. While the company relied on free snow tire changing in Michigan and free flat repairs in Arizona—the free flat service wouldn't expand nationally until 1994—Halle and Von Voigtlander continued to look for ads that would draw floor traffic. In 1975, the company hired Robert Natkin Advertising in Scottsdale to come up with its first television commercial, and Natkin delivered what would become the longest-running commercial in the history of the medium.

The ten-second advertisement shows an old woman heaving a tire through a Discount Tire store window. The voiceover announcer intones, "If ever you're not satisfied with one of our tires, please feel free to bring it back. Thank you, Discount Tire Company."

The ad has run hundreds of thousands of times in the more than thirty-five years since it first aired, and it was recognized by the Guinness Book of World Records in 2005 as the longest continuously running ad in television history. Only one customer in that time has taken the invitation literally, tossing a tire through the window of a store in Wyoming, Michigan, a suburb of Grand Rapids.

The brief and direct advertisement distilled the company's message effectively, according to Halle. Every transaction at every store involves tires or wheels, but what the company is selling is customer service. If customers aren't happy, they won't come back.

Although Halle was enjoying the sunshine in Arizona, he continued to make his presence known as the majority shareholder in Michigan and flew back frequently to check out the stores in the company's larger region. Halle was a management-by-exception type of leader, relying on his people to do the job they were hired to do and stepping in only when something was askew.

Management by exception creates both risks and rewards. The right person will strive to justify the trust placed in him, while the wrong person will simply take more time to be discovered. Soon after setting up shop in Arizona, Halle learned that one of his long-tenured managers was stealing from the company, bringing inventory home and selling it on the side. Halle confronted the betrayer and the situation turned violent. Halle hadn't been in a physical altercation since mustering out of the service, but he lost his temper and thrashed his now-fired manager, earning a lawsuit for his troubles. It was an embarrassment to the now-established business leader, who suddenly had much to lose, but it might also have put the final nail in the coffin for Halle's temper. Although he would certainly have moments of anger in the future, he became increasingly adept at keeping his temper under control.

Today, it is rare to find anyone below the senior management ranks who has seen Halle in a state of pique. While he will express his dissatisfaction openly to his senior managers, he keeps the tone low-key enough to reach only its intended target, ensuring that no innocent bystanders get caught in the crossfire.

Notably, the betrayal by his store manager didn't change Halle's willingness to manage by exception. Although he would be betrayed by a handful of people over time, he focused on the betrayals as the exception and loyalty as the norm. As a result, he continued to trust the next person he hired, expecting and usually receiving the best from that person.

Halle held himself to the same standards he required of others. When he and Gerry put their first Arizona home on the market, he agreed to one offer before receiving a second offer for $50,000 more. While the first offer was still oral, Halle bypassed the opportunity to sell at a higher price.

"I figured, if I would go back on my word for $50,000 today, then maybe I'd do the same thing for $50 later on," he remembers. "It just wasn't worth it."

As the company and its stores began to post more substantial earnings, Halle also began to reward his managers more generously, initiating quarterly bonuses for store managers in the mid-1970s. While he would no longer cede ownership in the company, he was increasingly willing to distribute cash to the people who were making his business a success.

As the company grew, travel between the Arizona and Michigan regions began to wear on Halle. Although he had begun traveling first class on commercial flights, constant travel was fatiguing at best. He found his solution while waiting for a tennis court at the La Jolla Shores condominium development in 1977. Halle's tennis partners—Eller, Galvin and Lyon—were waiting for a court and discussing the value of corporate jets. Halle had been considering a new investment in apartment buildings in the Phoenix area, but the talk intrigued him.

Since his first flight from home in Michigan to Camp Pendleton in California, Halle had loved air travel. Although Gerry squeezed his hand to the breaking point on their first descent into the mountainside airport at Aspen, the couple had begun taking flights like other people took taxis. After listening to the stories from his more-established peers, Halle decided to skip the investment in Phoenix apartment buildings and buy his first jet—a Cessna Citation.

"That changed my life," Halle says. "Airplanes have allowed me to do all of this travel efficiently and quickly all over the country. And the staff on the plane has nowhere to go, so we can focus. We couldn't have grown this way taking commercial flights."

Besides, having a corporate plane would be very, very cool.

Halle was quick to share his enjoyment of private jet travel with his employees. As Gary Van Brunt and Steve Fournier built revenues in Arizona, Halle decided it would be fun to reward them with an airborne outing. In 1979, he sent Van Brunt, Fournier and Holman from Phoenix to Orange County, California—for dinner. The next morning, he arrived at work early and called his friends in as soon as they got to the office, giddier than they were about their experience, according to Holman.

Eventually, the flight on a company jet would be a standing commitment for Halle. When any store reaches $200,000 in monthly sales, Halle sends a company plane to take the full-time employees and their significant others on an outing. The flight might take them from Detroit to Mackinac Island or from Salt Lake City to Los Angeles. For most employees, it would be the first time on a corporate jet.

"These are young people in the stores and to get a day of jetting with their wives or their friends, that's exciting," Halle says, visibly excited by the idea. "On a private jet! Most people never get on one."

Since the first incentive flight in 1983, Discount Tire has flown more than four thousand employees on these trips. Halle has resisted suggestions that he raise the threshold level for a corporate flight to reflect the impact of inflation. The flight is both a reward and an incentive, in his mind, and the sooner he incentivizes the people in his stores, the better.

"Someone will tell me we should increase the incentive sales level because tires cost more now," Halle notes, "but my response is always the same: 'Why didn't you mention that idea when it was your turn to take the flight?'"

Successful expansion in Michigan and Arizona continued to build both cash flow and earnings for the teenaged company, enabling Halle and Von Voigtlander to grow to thirty-one stores—twenty in Michigan and eleven in Arizona—by the end of 1978. Revenue that year surged 47 percent to $27 million, and the regional upstart was getting recognition as a company to watch. On a per-store basis, overhead remained low and volumes were high, enabling new stores to achieve profitability quickly in most cases.

There was no question that the company was succeeding and both Halle and Von Voigtlander were becoming increasingly wealthy. Now, nearly twenty years after Bruce Halle had decided to sell tires instead of day-old bread or factory-second shoes, he and his partner were ready to double down on their expansion program.

GOING FOR BROKE

As the company built its momentum and track record, Halle and Von Voigtlander decided to accelerate their pace of growth. Although Discount Tire was not yet a household name, its combination of low prices and surprisingly good customer service was proving to be sustainable. Bob Holman was lining up larger lines of credit, and vendors were more aggressive when courting their business.

In 1979, Halle was optimistic enough to buy a second jet, an eight-seat Lear 35, and repositioned the six-passenger Citation in Michigan for use by Von Voigtlander. Although the distances between stores were generally small in each of the two regions, having two jets made a statement to both employees and competitors: Discount Tire had arrived. Halle and Von Voigtlander decided to bring that message home to the entire industry when the National Tire Dealers and Retreaders Association held its 1979 annual meeting in Discount Tire's home area—Detroit.

Halle and Von Voigtlander brought a slew of managers to the conference as a way of demonstrating the size of their organization. Dave Fairbanks and Al Olsen researched wardrobe options and outfitted each manager in a navy blue Discount Tire blazer, white shirt and tan Sansabelt slacks. Discount Tire's team presented a sharp contrast to the more casual appearance of most tire retailers—small or large—at Detroit's then-new Renaissance Center.

Maury and Jay Isaacson feted the Discount Tire team in a reception at the top of the hotel, where Gerry Halle made a sport of transferring fuzz from her sweater to the navy blue jackets of her spiffy companions. While the Isaacsons' soiree was important recognition for Discount Tire, other, more exclusive parties beckoned.

Gary Van Brunt, Jack Chambers, Dave Fairbanks, Al Olsen and John Arthurs crashed the Michelin tire party, only to be undone by their upscale attire. A Michelin executive noticed the word *discount* on the jackets, sniffed that Michelin never discounted its product and had them ejected from the party. Within the next decade, Discount Tire would become one of Michelin's most important customers in the United States.

Undaunted, the merry band set its sights on Goodyear's hospitality suite, where the company hosted an event that would never include an off-brand retailer like Discount Tire. Even though the company was a substantial customer of Lee Tire, a Goodyear subsidiary, Discount Tire was not in Goodyear's league.

As Van Brunt and his comrades tried to convince the security guard that they had simply misplaced their invitations, they attracted the attention of Bill Sweatt, then a vice president at Goodyear. Sweatt looked the men over and invited them in for a drink. Sweatt was impressed with both the spirit and the presentation of the nattily-attired tire jockeys. "They looked sharp, physically and mentally," he says simply.

In 1980, Goodyear would send Sweatt to restore profitability to its Lee Tire subsidiary, which was in danger of shutting its plants. Lee Tire was selling a disproportionate share of its products to wholesalers, missing the opportunity for higher margins available through direct sale to retailers. When he took over as president, Sweatt directed his team to shift the balance more to retailers. Tom Greenwood, vice president in charge of Lee's Monarch brand, was already a supplier to Discount Tire. He thought the upstart retailer had growth potential and suggested a meeting.

"I said, 'Why don't you bring them in?'" Sweatt remembers. "When they came over, there was Bruce and Ted and Gary and Al. And when Gary and Al walked in, I realized I had already met them the year before in the hospitality suite. I asked Bruce what their plans were and he said they had started in Ann Arbor, expanded to Arizona and wanted to continue doing expansion as they could afford it."

Halle impressed Sweatt as "a guy who appeared to be going where he wanted and had the ability to probably do what he thought he could do."

Like the Isaacson brothers, Harry Regetz and Sister Marie Ellen before him, Sweatt would prove to be a key mentor and friend to Halle. Sensitive to the changes in the tire industry and the rising importance of independent dealers, he was anxious to identify the strongest partners for the coming years.

Several years prior to his move to Lee Tire, Sweatt had been in charge of Goodyear's retail stores on the West Coast. There, he had been accustomed to a service mix that included oil changes, brakes and other maintenance. When he visited Arizona to check out Discount Tire, he was both surprised and impressed by the high-volume operation that focused solely on tires. High turnover more than compensated for the lower gross margin—a lesson learned nearly fifteen years earlier at Dave Fairbanks's store—and customer satisfaction rose with the reduced wait times.

"I was a stickler on cleanliness of stores and I was also impressed with the overall housekeeping," Sweatt continues. "There wasn't paper all over the darn place. The store manager knew exactly where the heck everything was."

Sweatt and Halle would build a strong bond as Lee and Discount Tire expanded their relationship. Sweatt saw in Halle the kind of entrepreneurship and relationships with employees that would stand the test of time. Halle saw Sweatt as "a quality, ethical guy" and one of the polished gentlemen who always had impressed him.

Halle noticed that Sweatt was consistent in thanking others for making him a success and refrained from speaking ill of others—two traits that Halle admired and worked to emulate over the years.

Eventually, Sweatt would create a major opening for Halle's team as he returned to the corporate office at Goodyear and convinced his colleagues to begin meeting with fast-growing retailers who had been kept at a distance until then.

"I went to see the chairman and president of Goodyear and I suggested—I strongly suggested—I said, 'You know, you gentlemen aren't aware of some of the people in the tire business in the United States,'" Sweatt says. The chairman at the time, Charles J. Pilliod Jr., had been international head of the business and was exposed to more of the distribution network while in Europe, so he was open to the idea. "It was really wonderful exposure to Goodyear, for them to meet Bruce and the Discount folks, as well as for Bruce and his people to meet them."

Goodyear wouldn't begin selling tires directly to Discount Tire until 1994. As of the first day of that relationship, Discount Tire became Goodyear's largest dealer. Despite the delay between the party-crashing incident and the direct sales agreement, Halle believes Sweatt's aegis was a strong motivator for him and the company.

"The recognition that Bill gave us by introducing us to a lot of other people, just gave us the confidence that we were something," Halle says. "Nothing drastic changed overnight, but it was just a support system, just somebody that could walk into Goodyear headquarters and say, 'Discount Tire Company is okay.'"

Even if Goodyear executives in Akron didn't recognize the fact in 1979, Halle and Von Voigtlander knew they were building a quality operation. Corporate jets notwithstanding, the company's cost structure was relatively lean at the store level. Interest rates were high, but credit was readily available.

Why not bet it all on an audacious expansion program?

At the end of their second decade in business, Halle and Von Voigtlander announced a plan to open twenty-five stores per year over each of the following four years. They'd finance their growth by borrowing as much as 90 percent of the opening cost of each new outlet and then, as inflation increased the value of the underlying property, they would refinance to get the capital to open additional sites.

It was the kind of risk Halle had taken in buying a house while still in college and in borrowing $5,000 to invest in Bill DiDonato's distribution business. It was also the kind of risk Halle would never accept today, but he was more fearless, possibly reckless, in those years. He thought the company's momentum was strong and sustainable, which made it less risky than it appeared.

It wasn't. In fact, Halle and Von Voigtlander were literally betting the store. On a balance sheet, real estate is always listed at its purchase price, not at its appreciated value. By obtaining loans based on rising property values, Discount Tire ended up with a balance sheet that made the company appear bankrupt—with far more debts than the assets to cover them. While bankers recognized and lent money against the market value of the properties, the company was vulnerable to any decline in those values. If property prices fell or credit markets dried up, as would happen in 2008–2009, or if new stores failed to generate the cash flow of their established peers, the entire business could be gone within as little as a year's time.

Confident that they had found the magic formula for successful expansion, Halle and Von Voigtlander announced that Dave Fairbanks would be moving to Denver in 1980 to open the company's third region. His transfer and the ambitious expansion plan were a shock to the system, according to Al Olsen, who was assisting Fairbanks in overseeing the Michigan stores at that time.

Creation of a new region meant much more than the addition of new stores, in Olsen's mind. It also meant that the Michigan stores would experience a substantial drain of talent as Fairbanks looked to staff the Colorado stores with experienced Discount Tire managers. Part of the company's strength flowed from the loyal managers who had joined the team and thrived in the stores. Taking them out of their stores and moving them to new locations would break up the teams, and it could be hugely challenging to find more of the right people quickly enough to make the gamble succeed.

"As Dave is going to Colorado, I have nineteen stores in Michigan and one in Indiana," Olsen says. "Now I need to fill a pipeline."

The company invaded Colorado with the acquisition of E.J. Reynolds Tire Company, which operated eight stores in the state. While it was difficult to convince Arizona store managers or assistant managers to relocate to Colorado, the move was appealing to up-and-comers in the Michigan and Indiana stores. The drain that Olsen feared in his region was beginning in earnest.

Olsen hired two recruitment agencies and started visiting area colleges to find the bright young guys he'd need to feed the rapid growth plan. He instituted group interviews and role-playing to identify people with the necessary customer focus.

"Everybody that I was hiring, I advised them that if you have a special someone, partner or wife, she's gotta know," Olsen reports. "Don't say 'Yes, I accept coming on board' unless you understand you're going to leave Michigan in four or five months after you start with us."

After Colorado, Discount Tire started opening stores in California, Nevada, Oregon, Texas and New Mexico. The company didn't succeed in opening twenty-five stores per year, but Discount Tire tripled its footprint from thirty-six units at the end of 1979 to 110 at the end of 1984. Revenue grew at an even faster rate, rising 270 percent to $126 million in 1984 from $34 million just five years earlier.

By that time, Discount Tire was the third-largest independent tire dealer in the country, behind Big O and Les Schwab. With the addition of thirty more stores in 1985, the company jumped to the top of the heap.

Although it would be years before Goodyear would fully embrace the company, Discount Tire was courted heavily by other major manufacturers. While the off-brand retailer had been selling private labels made for the Isaacson brothers' World Tire in the earlier years, Discount Tire began to develop its own private labels directly with manufacturers.

In return for the generosity shown to him, Halle continued buying from World Tire until the business was sold in the 1980s. As the company grew, however, direct purchasing became both possible and more profitable.

In 1982, the company began selling its proprietary Arizonian tire, modeled in part after the private-label Californian tire offered by that state's largest independent dealer, Sam Winston. Ironically, freight costs precluded initial sales of the Arizonian in Arizona, limiting most of its market to Michigan and Indiana, where it was made by BF Goodrich.

In 1985, Halle established what would become a very close relationship with Francois Michelin, who was seeking strategic partners to expand sales of Michelin radial tires. Radial tires were developed by Michelin in 1948, but it would be decades before they were accepted widely in the United States. Michelin needed to establish a strong retail beachhead in the United States, but the company was not accustomed to dealing with discounters. Meanwhile, the higher price of radials, compared to bias-ply tires, presented its own challenges for the low-price retailer. Still, the market was moving and Halle needed to follow. He and Francois Michelin hit it off, and a long-term partnership was established.

Halle began to emerge as a leader in the retailing industry. Although he wouldn't seek a leadership role in any trade groups, his reputation as an ethical and successful entrepreneur won respect from both vendors and competitors. Shel Diller, a tire wholesaler who met Halle shortly after the move from Michigan, invited him to join a buying group that Diller had set up.

Halle didn't buy much from Diller's Empco distribution business, but he joined the buying group Diller formed to negotiate with General Tire and a few other companies. Tires Plus founder Tom Gegax, one of the retailers who joined the buying group, operated in Minnesota and regularly told Halle to stay out of that state. Discount Tire would not open its Minnesota region until 2001, after Gegax had sold his business to Bridgestone/Firestone.

Diller says Halle's influence was clear in the buying group's 1986 meeting with General Tire in New York. Halle, Diller and a number of other retailers joined the breakfast session with Gil Neal, who was president of General Tire at the time.

"I'm the spokesman, mostly, and we're trying to talk about the reasons he should drop the price," Diller remembers. "I was talking until I was blue in the face. Bruce was sitting there rather quietly and I kept talking and talking and I didn't know if I was getting anywhere and then Bruce said, 'Gil, I think you need to do this,' and Gil agreed. That was Bruce's influence."

While Halle's star was rising, his relationship with Von Voigtlander began to fray. The two had started out working together like a pair of matched oxen, pulling in unison and sharing equally in the labor. As the company grew, however, Halle began to feel that Von Voigtlander was spending too much time on outside ventures and investments and covering too many expenses with the company's dime. Twice, Halle would pull the second jet out of Michigan, depriving his minority partner of its use. In 1994, Halle would buy back shares from Von Voigtlander to help him cover losses on a failed investment outside the company.

The rift was still largely invisible to most employees in the early 1980s, but it was clear that Halle was consolidating his leadership role in Arizona, creating a corporate office in 1985 and moving all administrative functions that were still in Michigan out to Scottsdale in 1987.

As the company's fortunes grew and the expansion gamble paid off, Halle began to pay forward to more of his managers with higher bonuses and more lavish parties. The impetuous decision to fly Fournier, Holman and Van Brunt to California for dinner in 1979 led to incentive flights awarded when stores first reach $200,000 in sales in one month. The 1981 fishing trip that Bill Sweatt offered as a prize for selling Discount Tire's private-label RoadHugger brand morphed into a three-day, Discount Tire-sponsored extravaganza for upwards of three hundred employees at Lake Tahoe.

As the company opened new stores and regions, *Tire Business* magazine ranked Discount Tire at the top of its industry, with 201 company-owned stores and $311 million in revenue for 1988.

The business was operating more and more efficiently as well-trained managers spread out across the country to maintain its customer-focused discipline. The Washington State region opened in 1987 and Florida was added in 1989, the same year the hundred largest privately held companies in Arizona named Discount Tire the Most Admired Company in the state.

Halle recruited Christian Roe, who had been one of his primary commercial bankers, to add depth to the finance department in 1988, and Halle and Roe began to obtain capital for expansion directly from tire companies.

Ironically, as the company's reputation as a disciplined and profitable retailer was growing, Halle lost some of his focus in the 1980s, fiddling with the model that had made the company successful.

As the 1980s began, Discount Tire started offering replacement batteries as a product expansion, reasoning that battery replacement is a simple process like changing a tire. However, a drained battery is often the result of another problem, such as a faulty alternator, and Discount Tire wasn't in the business of fixing alternators. Simply offering new batteries disappointed more customers than it pleased, leading Halle to drop the program. In 1988, Halle opened a buying club, Tires Plus Club, in California, reasoning that other buying clubs were successful and there was room for a club dedicated to automotive products. Again, he was wrong. The huge store required far more staff than its revenues could justify and, three years after opening his 35,000-square-foot store in California, Halle backed off on his costly experiment.

"Here's what we didn't realize," explains Jim Silhasek, chief corporate counsel. "Consumers don't know much about tires, so they have to rely on someone else to explain what they need. So we needed many more people than we had planned for, just to explain the differences and what tires would work out best. That meant more people on the floor, higher costs and a very inefficient operation."

The experiment was far from a total loss for the company. Tires Plus Club started a mail-order business, running ads in trade magazines and assembling a telemarketing group. When Halle closed the megastore, the telemarketing group moved to Scottsdale and grew profitably.

"At that time, nobody had heard of e-commerce and the Internet was not a great big deal," Halle remembers. "Now, along comes the Internet and e-commerce and we have the people in telemarketing, plus a lot of stores. We were already positioned before a lot of other people, because of our telemarketing."

By 1994, the telemarketing business had morphed into Discount Tire Direct, which operates largely online and ships tires and wheels across the country. Entering the market early, Discount Tire also snapped up two attractive URLs—www.tire.com and www.tires.com—as it launched its websites. Over the years, Halle has been approached about selling the URLs, but he has declined the opportunity.

None of the missteps in the 1980s proved disastrous for the growing company, just as the continued availability of credit and rising property values supported Halle's investment in new stores. While Halle was taking oversized risks and deviating from his successful business model, the company was being propelled forward by a growing team of average Joes who came to the company with no expectations, but were inspired by Halle and each other to achieve above-average results.

THE LOST BOYS

"I spent two years in junior college and I didn't have any direction. I didn't know what I wanted to do with my life," Gregg Olewinski notes.

"My dad thought I would party too much in college if I didn't have a job," Ron Archer explains.

"I just came in because I needed a regular paycheck," Tim Ehinger admits.

"I was the youngest of three. By the time it was my turn to graduate from high school, my mom told me there were no college funds left," Vern Roberson recalls.

"I thought I wanted a corporate job at a bank or something," Al Hatfield remembers.

Olewinski, Archer, Ehinger, Roberson and Hatfield are all regional vice presidents at Discount Tire Company. Each arrived by mistake. None regrets the error.

The management ranks at Discount Tire—from the stores to the regional offices and the corporate operations team—are populated by people who never heard of the company while they were going to school and never, ever thought they'd spend their lives as tire salesmen.

"I thought this was a really good opportunity to go to a company, learn a bit about retail and management and then I'd quit, realize the American Dream and start my own company," recalls Larry Allen. Thirty-five years later, Allen is vice president of the Houston region, responsible for roughly $350 million in revenue at nearly eighty stores. "It turns out I didn't have to start my own company to realize the American Dream," he says today.

Vern Roberson was working his way through college in 1981 when an employment agency arranged a "management trainee" interview for what turned out to be a tire-changing job at Discount Tire. "The manager of the first store I worked at was driving a black Corvette, and it turned out he never finished high school. I thought, 'This guy is living the dream.' If he could do it, I figured, so could I."

The day he was promoted to assistant manager at his store, Roberson bought himself a red Corvette. In 2002, he was promoted to vice president of the New Mexico/West Texas region and now heads up the Georgia region.

The prototypical backstory of a Discount Tire executive includes a lack of specific goals, average or lower-than-average grades and minimal expectations of the job or the company. Most applicants are looking for nothing more than a steady paycheck and, maybe, a place to bide their time while they figure out what to do with their lives.

In many respects, they look just like Bruce Halle.

Halle was the original "lost boy" at the time he prepared to open his first store. He didn't have much of a plan other than putting food on the table. He was willing to work hard, but had no particular skills. He had completed college, but didn't exactly burn up the track on his way to the top of his class.

If Discount Tire had existed at the end of 1959, it would have been the ideal place for Bruce Halle to find a job. Instead, he had to build his opportunity from zero.

Discount Tire is built around *Who*, as in "*Who* will make us successful?" Customers can buy tires anywhere, and most customers cannot tell the difference between one tire and another. For a company to excel in a commodity market, product differentiation is a non-starter. Improve the customer experience, however, and brand value explodes.

Halle would change the experience early by offering free mounting of snow tires. Later, he offered free flat repairs and introduced one of the first tire warranty certificates that covered risks not included in the manufacturers' warranties. Every full-time employee has the authority to give away a tire, or a set of tires, when a down-and-out customer needs some extra help or a specific situation suggests that the customer should get a break.

When Halle started in 1960, giving customers a break on a warranty or changing snow tires at no charge were substitutes for advertising and marketing, which he couldn't afford. He had time on his hands, at first, so providing free labor had no extra cost. Over time, free services brought in paying customers, convincing Halle that *free* can be very profitable.

Still, it takes more than offering something for nothing to make customers happy. Even free services have no impact when the person delivering the service does it grudgingly or shames the customer, according to Al Hatfield, vice president in Orange County, California. If the customer thinks the employee is working to make things right, it's a victory. If the employee decides to win a debate, the company loses.

The search for people with the right attitude led directly to the lost boys. The cadre of young men—and they are almost always men—joining the company often shared a certain lack of focus in life. What separated the keepers from the rest of the pack was a willingness to work hard and to find that focus as part of a team. The team is critical, because the team is bigger than the individual, and a person who believes in the team will often be committed to serving others—including both the company and its customers.

Hatfield says the people who succeed at Discount Tire are the ones who understand how to make the customer happy. It's not enough to honor a warranty or fix a flat at no charge; the employee must show that he really wants to do it.

"They have no issues giving away a tire. There's no cost to it. But sometimes they think they need to get their point across first, which is backwards. Get the point across later and take care of the problem first," Hatfield says.

Because the individual employee is the "secret sauce" in Discount Tire's success, the company is built around the worker more than it is designed around the customer. Hire the wrong people and you'll find that you can't beat them hard enough to make them treat customers well. Hire the right people and no beatings are necessary.

"Happy employees make happy customers, but happy customers don't always make for happy employees," explains Tim Ehinger, vice president in the Detroit region. "So we need to find a way for employees to believe in what they do. It's in our mission statement to be the best and to care for and cultivate our people. When we show our people how much we care, that's where the magic happens and they become passionate about what they're doing. Nothing happens until you sell something, so you have to make sure you have happy people who are motivated or you won't sell a thing."

Kevin Easter links the right attitude to the most basic of value systems. "The Golden Rule and the Ten Commandments are what this company is, but it's not put out that way," he notes. "Mr. Halle is the most spiritual man I've ever met, but he's never said a word to me about religion. It's all in how he lives. We're in business to make money, but the way you let Mr. Halle down isn't by not selling tires, but by not taking care of the people."

Most important, Easter says, the company lives up to its commitment to reward people who focus on customer satisfaction. "You're told to take care of customers, that customers are important. That happens at every company," Easter notes. "But this is the first company I've seen that doesn't punish you for taking care of the customer. In fact, you get in trouble if you don't."

Across the company, the people who've succeeded focus on the same issues and the same values in describing what makes the company work. The lost boys who can see their success as dependent on serving others tend to rise at Discount Tire.

"The fact is that we are empowered from day one to take care of any customer for whatever reason, to keep them safe and to gain a customer for life," says Bill Wendell, vice president of the Minnesota region. "It's nurtured over time: manners, politeness, doing what's right, just kindness and honesty. So much in our business is the perception that we're automotive, so maybe we can't be trusted or our locations are dirty, but once you get them in the front door, and they see our clean buildings and our people, it's not so much that we're selling tires but a matter of making friends over time. You want repeat customers, people who refer us to family, friends, coworkers . . . we want to make them customers for life."

The right person can be trained to channel his energies toward customer satisfaction, but a person who isn't a team player is very unlikely to make the connection. The turnover rate is more than 80 percent for part-timers, reflecting the rigors of tire changing, but turnover drops to a minuscule 2 percent for store managers.

"It's very much like the military in the sense that you feel like you are a part of something bigger than yourself," says Ed Kaminski, regional vice president in San Antonio. "I was blessed with the opportunity to serve in the military and got the chance to experience the love, bonding and trust that come with that. Discount Tire is very much the same way."

A sense of belonging is one of the employee benefits at Discount Tire, one with strong appeal to the type of people the company wants to attract. Delivering on that promise requires a commitment by the company as well as its employees.

"We're a promote-from-within company," says Ron Archer. "Everybody knows that in this company you start at ground level. Look at all our vice presidents, our senior vice presidents, all the way to Tom Englert, our CEO. They all started out in the same place. We've been around fifty years and we've never had a layoff."

Discount Tire's promote-from-within policy offers a brass ring to everyone who starts as a part-time tire tech. While it is possible to get a job in finance, law and other specialty areas without busting tires, the path upward in operations is open only to tire jockeys. Promotions are competitive, but the competition is always among peers.

"If I were to bring someone in at a high level without having worked in the stores, I may as well get in my car, drive around to the stores and slap every one of the guys in the face—because that's literally what I'd have done to them. And I would never do that," Halle says.

The promote-from-within policy has enormous power among Discount Tire employees, not merely due to its perceived fairness but also for the parallels it creates with Bruce Halle's path. Much as Halle played the role of surrogate dad when his own father was gone from home, his executive team will often cite a mandate to "be the dad" for their own employees.

The mandate is often literal. Several Discount Tire executives have sons and daughters in the business, and Dave Fairbanks, Halle's college friend and manager of store number four, has both a son, who was named Bruce in honor of his good friend, and grandsons working at Discount Tire. For many, the company's ability to attract and inspire lost boys is also a personal benefit.

"As a manager, I've had parents tell me how much Discount Tire has helped their child, and I dismissed this. We didn't do anything special, it's just what we do," says Kevin Easter. "When my own sixteen-year-old son went to work at Discount Tire, I found out what other parents had thanked me for. My son was not a strong student and I worried about what life had in store for him. Over the years, the various managers he worked for treated my son as their own. I watched my son change before my very eyes into a very responsible adult. As a parent, I went to these managers and thanked them for helping my son grow."

Easter notes that his son followed the same path that he himself had followed on the way to finding a niche at Discount Tire. "I'm a three-time college dropout," he says. "I tried three times and hated it each time."

Discount Tire has succeeded, in part, by exceeding the generally low expectations that both customers and employees might have about the tire business. Customers don't expect quick turnaround, clean bathrooms or free repairs. New employees don't expect a lucrative career, team membership and a company that worries about their families.

"That's what makes Discount Tire great," Ray Winiecke, San Diego vice president, says. "We didn't bring in all those college guys to show us how to do it, but we've learned and grown together and shared the experience of building the company together."

REVERSAL OF FORTUNE

As the bet-it-all plan for rapid expansion paid off and Bruce Halle gained increasing renown in his industry and adopted state, he and Gerry increased their travels, and Halle's gifts to his high-school sweetheart became increasingly lavish.

"Bruce would do anything for Gerry," says Gary Van Brunt. "She never really asked for anything, but Bruce was always there doing things for Gerry—'Let's go buy some clothes,' so they're off to New York to buy some dresses. He just wanted to do things for Gerry."

Bruce shared the wealth with his parents as well, buying them a house for their retirement in Florida and providing them with the comforts that Fred Halle had never been able to provide through his own labors.

"Bruce said that if he ever made any money in his life, he would take care of his mother and his dad," recalls Charlotte Fournier, Molly's niece and mother of Discount Tire COO Steve Fournier. Halle lived up to that promise, taking care of his mom until she died in 1985 in Florida. After Molly died, Bruce moved Fred Halle out to Arizona and bought a place for him to live nearer to Bruce's family.

Frederick J. Halle began his new life in Sun City, Arizona, still the fun-loving, bigger-than-life idol that Bruce had looked up to as a boy in Berlin, New Hampshire. Taking care of his father, like taking care of his mother, was never a question to Bruce, even though it was sometimes a challenge to keep pace with his dad's new adventures.

"Well, Dad didn't get an Arizona license. He had an expired Florida one, and he let the insurance lapse on his car," Halle remembers. "He's going down the road in Sun City and the police pull him over and now we have to go out to a justice of the peace in Wickenburg. So [General Counsel] Jim Silhasek and I and Dad go out there, all in suits, and it's the justice of the peace in Wickenburg and this is his little kingdom. He looks down at the front row and there's three guys in suits. And he says, 'Oh, we've got an attorney here?' Dad and I said we weren't attorneys, but Jim says he is, and Jim gets up and addresses this judge like it's the Supreme Court. He really lays it on. It was really cool."

In the end, the judge fined Fred Halle $600, which Bruce considered a bargain in light of the kinds of fines the judge was throwing out that day. Next, he took his dad to get a new license, but Fred couldn't read any of the letters on the eye test.

"I said, 'Dad, are these your glasses?' and he said, 'No, I got these at Walgreens but they're okay.' So we take him to the eye doctor for a new set of glasses and we come back and he passes that. So now he has to take the driving test and he goes around and comes back and he can't pass that test, so we went to take the test in Sun City, where they deal with older people. But first, I had someone follow the drivers around on the route so we could have my dad rehearse where they go, where they turn left, where they turn right, where they park and all this. And then he takes the test and passes. And by the way, that took about four months."

Halle laughs at the craziness of the experience, but it's the least he could do for the larger-than-life guy who taught him how to box.

Caring for his parents represented a repayment for Bruce, but it also tied into his commitment to take care of his wife in a way that his dad had not been able to achieve for Molly. Geraldine Konfara Halle, a smart and elegant woman, would not have to wait until she was in her sixties to enjoy her life fully. Halle took pride in buying gifts for Gerry, doting on her and giving her a life he had been unable to give to his mother.

Halle's father was his primary role model as a husband and father, but Bruce's personality had much of Molly grafted into it. Bruce loved to play pranks and have fun, and he enjoyed the physicality of life that Fred Halle personified. Like Molly, however, he was a bit more shy, more reserved, less likely to seek the limelight. Halle enjoyed being one of the guys but didn't feel the need, or sometimes, the worthiness, to be THE guy. Gerry had proved to be as nearly perfect a match for Bruce as friends and family could imagine. He saw her as smart and polished, capable of fitting in with the lost boys who made up his team at Discount Tire and the corporate chieftains who became their neighbors and friends in Arizona. She managed the household while Bruce worked sixty- to seventy-hour weeks, first in college and later at the stores. She served as sounding board and pep squad as Bruce brought home cash, stories and problems from the store. And she continued to serve as the Discount Tire Mom, making both the men from the stores and their wives feel welcome, as if they had a second family.

"Gerry wasn't impressed with herself and she wasn't impressed by others, either," says longtime friend Cynthia Tubbs. Cynthia's husband, Jim, had sold Bruce a number of store locations in Arizona, and the couples became fast friends. When Halle bought his first plane, they flew with Cynthia and Jim to Jackson Hole, Wyoming, for the night. "Money enabled her to do lots of things she might not have been able to do otherwise, but it didn't change her," Tubbs remembers.

In 1987, Halle set up Gerry and his daughters in their own business, a children's clothing store called Spoiled Rotten in La Jolla, California. Both Susan and Lisa were living in California by then and Gerry thought the store would be a great way to spend more time with her daughters and source cute clothes for Bruce Jr.'s daughters, Audrey and Ashley. In the same year, Bruce outbid several of his peers to buy an espresso machine once used to make a cup of coffee for Pope John Paul II during his visit to Arizona. He had no interest in paying $14,000 for a $900 espresso machine, but Gerry said she wanted it. Done deal.

Gerry and Bruce had broadened their vistas, both literally and figuratively, with a strong business arc to carry them forward. Both were fully committed not only to each other and to Catholicism, but also to their health. Although Bruce did not possess the most beneficial dietary habits—he has a semi-addiction to Costco hot dogs—the two played tennis, skied, pursued an active lifestyle and underwent annual health check-ups. Although Gerry had complained for some time about severe pain in her lower back, it was more than a year before doctors determined that she had stage-four ovarian cancer. By that time, the cancer had spread to her stomach and uterus. Gerry began chemotherapy while Bruce searched for a specialist who could reverse the irreversible.

In the battle that mattered more to him than any other, he would not succeed. Geraldine Konfara Halle died April 8, 1989. She was fifty-nine years old.

"They had quite a love affair, and my dad is such a caretaker," daughter Lisa says. "He loves fixing things and he just wasn't able to fix this and . . . he's such a Marine. He's going to power through this and he's going to make everything better. But this time it wasn't going to happen that way."

Father Ray Bucher, a family friend and religious adviser, recalls that Gerry was more concerned about her family than herself as she accepted the reality of her condition. Bucher says she proved to be both a positive example of how to live and, also, how to face the inevitable.

"What you take into dying is a reflection of how you lived, and she simply lived her life with great courage and hope," he recalls.

Halle set up his office at the hospital and would spend as much time as he could by Gerry's side. When she died at Scripps Memorial in San Diego, Bruce Halle returned home, alone, a broken man.

"It was just her attitude, her love, her support, her confidence in me, her encouragement," Halle relates. "We were married thirty-eight years and it was beautiful, just wonderful. She was just a great partner and never any big challenges, never any big problems, just a wonderful person. She had a perpetual smile on her face. She made you feel good just being in the room with her."

When Halle returned to his empty home, daughter Lisa stayed with him for a week, and his friends sought to console him, but he was not responsive. He threw himself more deeply into the work of the company, filling his emptiness with the details of selling tires. At night, though, he was likely to be home, alone, eating canned food for dinner, not interested in the outside world.

"Gerry and Bruce really grew up together," says Shel Diller, a close friend and longtime colleague of Halle's. "Their whole adult life was together and they were one person. All of Bruce's thoughts and everything were with Gerry. They were one person. I have never, ever seen a marriage like they had. Ever. Ever. God, they were one person."

Without his guide to the outside world, Halle retreated into his business and the company of a few close friends. He'd spend time in semi-retreat with Father Ray Bucher, who had officiated at Lisa's wedding and become a friend of Bruce and Gerry's. A devout Catholic, Halle argued with Father Ray about the mistake God had made in taking Gerry. Halle remained true to his faith but believed The Boss had not been true to Gerry—or to him.

Bruce Halle remained in mourning for the better part of two years, ensconced in his home in Paradise Valley or his retreat in Colorado. Slowly, he came out of his shell and began to return to many of his old activities, but only within a small circle of friends and, of course, Discount Tire. Strongly committed to the American Heart Institute, he agreed to serve as honorary chairman of their annual Heart Ball in 1992, but his appearances at charitable and social events were minimal.

Halle's return to normalcy was sidetracked dramatically in the spring of 1993. The Phoenix Suns were playing the Chicago Bulls in the NBA finals. Halle and Bruce Jr. flew to Chicago with Karl and Stevie Eller to watch the Suns lose their third of the first three games in the series. On the way home to Arizona, Halle stopped off in Snowmass, Colorado, to spend a few days while the Ellers and Bruce Jr. continued to Phoenix.

"I got up the next morning to ride a mountain bike up there, and I generally wore a helmet. I just didn't on that day for some reason. It was a trail that I rode all the time," Halle recalls matter-of-factly today. "I came off my bike and landed in some rocks. Didn't have a helmet on and I was in a short-sleeved shirt. I'm bleeding out of my head. I'm unconscious, a lot of skin gone, a broken collarbone, and I landed in some rock, but I must have crawled three or four feet because I was right in the trail, out of the rocks. So, I can't remember any of that. A young boy, a local boy who was riding his bike, spotted me and called the medics and they came and took me to Aspen Hospital. But I didn't wake up there. They kept me sedated and they moved me to Denver, to Swedish Hospital, and I woke up there."

In fact, Halle was nearly dead when the twelve-year-old boy happened upon him and called for help. Internal bleeding posed a major threat, but swelling of the brain from his head injury threatened permanent damage or death. The staff at Aspen Valley Hospital lacked the tools to provide complete treatment, so they kept Halle deeply sedated while arranging to transfer him to Swedish Medical Center in Denver.

"In Denver, my daughters Susan and Lisa were really something. They went to a Ralph Lauren store and bought sheets and pillowcases and all the beautiful stuff that he has and decorated my whole room. It was gorgeous," Halle says, willing to focus on every aspect of the experience except his brush with death. "Nurses and doctors in the hospital just wanted to come to my room to look at the interior, not at me."

Bruce Jr., who had already moved to California to open Discount Tire's operations in that state, called Dr. Ralph Lilly, a neurosurgeon and family friend, to oversee his father's care. Lilly had Halle transferred to Hermann Hospital in Houston, where Lilly practiced, both to provide more personal care for his friend and to insulate him from any demands of the office. Halle was a workaholic and Lilly knew he would want to get involved in the business before it was wise to do so.

Lilly had personal insight into Halle's recovery path, having suffered a brain injury himself a few years earlier. Lilly had met Halle shortly after the Halles moved to Arizona, and the two men would often ride together in the desert near their homes. Bruce and Gerry had been supportive of the ailing doctor after his injury and he was determined to return the favor.

For several days, it was not clear whether Halle would live, and it was a few weeks before anyone had an inkling of the condition he would be in when he returned to work. Back at the company, the shock was severe.

"There was no 'me' then," COO Steve Fournier remembers. By 1993, all corporate functions had already been consolidated in Arizona, and Ted Von Voigtlander was no longer involved in daily operations of the company. Bruce Jr., Gary Van Brunt, Tom Englert and Bob Holman were working at the corporate office as vice presidents, but there was no succession plan for Discount Tire and Halle had not created an estate plan.

Predictably, in hindsight, the culture kicked in to keep the company on an even keel. Discount Tire continued to operate as it had and the lost boys kept the business running smoothly until the boss could return.

Halle's recovery was relatively fast, in light of the injuries he had suffered, due to both the fortunate timing of his discovery by a local bicyclist and the years of physical conditioning that kept his heart and lungs in excellent condition. He returned to work with a vengeance later in 1993, determined to reestablish his personal momentum and prove to his team, and possibly to himself, that he was the same dynamic leader he had always been.

The accident had changed him, although not as much as is common after a brain injury.

He continued to suffer from vertigo and had trouble bending down to pick up a pen or tie his shoes, but that was the most visible difference in the company's founder. Close friends and family noticed, however, that Halle was more serious, less likely to play a physical gag or tell a joke. Far from somber, Halle was back to enjoying his life, grateful to be alive at all, but he was not as playful or jovial as he had been in the time before.

A person looking at the company's progress during the period of personal reversals might have no reason to suspect that any mishap had occurred. From the end of 1988 through the end of 1993, the company opened sixty-five stores and built revenues nearly 70 percent to $519 million.

Halle had upgraded to his largest jet so far, a Lockheed JetStar formerly belonging to Circus Circus Hotel & Casino in Las Vegas. Seeking a new pilot familiar with the larger plane, Halle found Bruce Gensemer, who had flown previously on Air Force One and was in the business of training pilots to fly the JetStar. Halle lured Gensemer to the company and opened a link that would eventually bring four Air Force One pilots to Discount Tire.

"When they quit working for the president, they come to work for the real president," says longtime friend Shel Diller.

The company had been named Arizona's Most Admired Company for a second and third time in 1990 and 1991, and Halle received Eastern Michigan University's Distinguished Alumni Award in 1993.

Halle had received a more meaningful honor, in a backhanded way, when Goodyear Chairman Stanley Gault called him in 1991. Halle had just moved Tom Englert to the corporate office to join Bruce Jr. as a senior vice president of store operations. Gault wanted to interview Englert for a position as head of Goodyear's retail tire stores and he wanted Halle's approval before approaching Englert. Halle said he would make no promises about the future and allowed Englert to check out the opportunity. It didn't take long for Englert to recognize the differences in culture and the political climate between the two companies and he opted to stay in the fold at Discount Tire. In 2004, Halle would promote Englert to chief executive officer.

To Halle, the incident was important on several levels. Gault's decision to obtain Halle's permission for the interview suggested an awareness of Discount Tire's importance in the industry, even if Goodyear was not yet selling directly to the company. Gault's interest in interviewing one of Halle's top managers was an indication that the talent pool at Discount Tire was at least on par with even the largest company. Englert's decision to stay where he was, with no promises from Halle, affirmed the strength of the bonds Discount Tire had established with its people.

The five-year period that began with Gerry's illness was personally unsettling for Bruce Halle as an individual. Professionally, it seemed, he and his lost boys were becoming a juggernaut.

RESET BUTTON

Todd Meerschaert had it made at Discount Tire after winning the keys to his first store. Just twenty-eight years old, he'd moved up from senior assistant to manager of the sole Discount Tire outpost in Lakewood, Colorado. He loved his job, loved the company and loved his location.

In 1990, though, life fell apart as the father of two preschool boys went through a painful divorce that also led to poor performance at work. Eventually, Tom Englert, then vice president of the Colorado region, sat down with Meerschaert for a life-changing conversation. Englert had talked to Meerschaert about his performance before, going so far as to buy him an alarm clock with the admonition to show up on time each day. Now, Englert was taking his store away and moving him to Boulder as an assistant manager.

Englert was hitting the reset button, a tool used regularly at Discount Tire to salvage the careers of good employees who hit a wall. In some cases, a family illness or other personal challenge will affect job performance. In many situations, though, the management team has simply made the mistake of promoting someone too early or moving a manager into the wrong job.

The reset button is a parable for the life of Bruce Halle; in fact, it's a normal pattern of life for most people. As a child, as a college student and as a new dad starting out in business, Halle hit dead ends and had to reboot several times. When his employees hit a wall in a similar way, he wants to give them the same opportunity he received.

Englert says the company gives its employees a wide circle of latitude and a small number of rules that allow no deviations. Steal from the company, abuse your employees, or mistreat customers, and the exit door is wide open, Englert says, "but if you're over-promoted, that's our mistake, not the employee's. We can't and shouldn't penalize people because they can't fulfill a role that we asked them to handle for us."

Englert's decision was a hard blow to his ambitious store manager, but "it gave me a good opportunity to refocus and rediscover how I felt about my position and how I had let that get away from me," Meerschaert says today.

After less than two years in Boulder, Meerschaert had regained his momentum. Regional Vice President Richard Kuipers, who had taken over as Colorado VP when Englert moved to the corporate office, promoted Meerschaert to manager of the Grand Junction store, which Meerschaert took as a sign of immense confidence.

"The amount of trust they gave me, to take over a store that was five hours away from the regional office, knowing I wouldn't get visited much by the regional office—that showed me they believed in me," Meerschaert says today. He repaid that trust by building sales and profitability and, later, transforming the Fort Collins store into the highest-profit shop in Colorado.

In 2000, Tom Englert called again, this time to promote him to assistant vice president of Discount Tire's San Diego region. In turn, Meerschaert has taken the opportunity to hit the reset button and salvage several of his own employees' careers.

"While I was running the Fort Collins store, my senior assistant left and we had two other assistants to consider as a replacement," he recalls. One person was excellent at details but not as strong on personality, while the other was stronger on personality and not as good at details. "Of course, we chose the person with the stronger personality, who didn't improve on details, while the detail guy got much better in dealing with people."

After about eight months, Meerschaert switched the two, demoting his senior assistant manager to an assistant level. Ultimately, the demoted assistant, Cleveland Muller, worked his way back, taking over as manager in the same Fort Collins store where he had been demoted years ago. Today, he tells a story similar to that of his former boss.

"It was hard from a pride standpoint," Muller says. "But I got a chance to go to other stores, get more training and be promoted again, first to senior assistant and then to store manager."

Meerschaert's current boss, San Diego vice president Ray Winiecke, ran into the reset button in the early 1990s while working as a senior assistant store manager in Troy, Michigan.

"I wasn't accountable and I didn't take ownership when I was left in charge of the store," Winiecke recalls today. "I didn't treat the job like I had much to do. I was in charge. I had made it. I wanted to be friends with the workers instead of supervising them, and if I didn't enjoy it, I didn't think of it as critical."

Both Winiecke and Meerschaert use their own experience as a training tool for newer guys coming up the ladder. "The choice is theirs," Winiecke says. "This is either going to be a blip on the radar or a trail of breadcrumbs leading back to them. I can tell them this has happened to me, and now the choice is theirs. What they choose to do now is up to them."

Meerschaert applies his own experience to help challenged managers change direction and get back on an upward arc at the company. The first step, of course, is getting those people to ask for help.

"When I teach a class, one of the first things I share is that I was demoted and re-promoted," Meerschaert says. "It always brings somebody up to talk to me at the end of the class. Guys who are struggling and in a room with a lot of guys they don't know won't necessarily stand up and make themselves vulnerable in front of a group, but they will if you make yourself vulnerable. It gives them a chance to connect with you, and it gives you a chance to talk to them. Whether they have been demoted or think they are in danger in one way or another, I can let them know it doesn't have to be the end of their career. It can be an opportunity to refocus."

Halle says the reset button is often a reflection of the company promoting an employee into a position where he is adding less value than before. Getting back to the earlier contribution level is the most important goal when that happens, he says.

"We've had people promoted to levels that were probably a mistake on our part, a level they couldn't achieve at. Nice people. Good people," Halle says. "And, of course, in our company, we don't let them loose and say good-bye. We reassign them and they're fine. Somebody who's a great manager, it doesn't mean he's going to be a great assistant vice president, and a good AVP won't necessarily be a good vice president. So how do you find that out? You give people an opportunity. You give them the chance to try it.

"Now, if you have a guy who's a great store manager and you promote him to AVP and it doesn't work for him, he's still a valuable person to you. Use him in some other way. We've got many years invested in him, maybe ten or fifteen years, whatever it is. You can't let that guy go. You'd be insane to do that."

The reset button also encourages employees to take appropriate risks, knowing they aren't putting their careers on the line when they agree to spearhead a new venture for the company.

When Halle established the Tires Plus Club in 1988, Jack Chambers, who had joined Halle in Michigan in 1967 and subsequently opened the Houston region for the company, was tapped to head the new venture. The experiment was a flop, and Halle pulled the plug three years later. Chambers kept his job, though, as Halle reassigned him to the corporate office to run the company's advertising programs.

Halle sees setbacks as opportunities to learn and grow. If people learn from their mistakes and recommit to achieving more—as Halle did in opening his first store—the company would be foolish to lose their contributions. The only way to adjust effectively, he says, is to have the right person in the right job, even if it takes a while to figure out which job that is.

THE WHIRLWIND

In hindsight, Halle sees his bicycle accident through much the same prism as he sees the reset button.

It happened.

Nobody died.

Move on.

Having received a reprieve from The Boss, Halle was ready to get back to living at full speed, both in his company and socially. He had begun dating, off and on, shortly before the bicycle accident, although he would often ask daughters Susan or Lisa, or both, to escort him to company parties or formal charity events.

At one such event, the Crisis Nursery gala in 1993, Susan noticed that her father was checking out Diane Cummings, a widow whose husband had succumbed to pancreatic cancer a year earlier. In fact, Bruce Halle had asked her out once before, but she had no interest in dating. Now, she seemed to be back in the social whirl and Halle was considering his options.

Of all the women in the room, possibly all the women in Phoenix, Diane Cummings seemed to be the least likely match for Bruce Halle. Born and raised in Chicago, she attended the private Latin School, married well, and lived as one of the polished people who always held a mystique—and distance—for him.

In 1935, Diane's grandparents, Anna and Joseph Lamprecht, emigrated from Germany as they grew concerned about the relatively new leadership of Adolf Hitler. The couple maintained their traditional culture in the United States, while Diane's mother, a teenager when they arrived in Chicago, gravitated immediately to the freedoms of her new country.

The split of cultures would define much of Diane's childhood. Her mother, Erica, would divorce Diane's father when Diane was four years old, and the family would move back into her grandparents' home in Chicago, where her grandfather would die the following year. Diane's mother maintained her emphasis on the social whirl, while her grandmother took on more of the traditional role of a mother.

"My grandmother taught me how to cook and bake and clean and all the stuff she thought a young girl should know," Diane recalls. "My mother taught me how to put on makeup and dress smartly."

In 1952, when Diane was just ten, Erica married Eddie Meyers, a well-to-do Chicagoan who introduced Erica and her daughter to a decidedly upscale lifestyle. Still, he insisted that Diane take summer jobs and keep her own checkbook, learning essential skills that might be needed later in life.

"I worked in traffic court one year, in City Hall another year, and one year I had to answer questions about the census," Diane recalls. "I realized I loved working. I liked getting up and having something to do. Eddie gave me my work ethic. If I had nowhere to go for the rest of my life but have lunch with other women and play tennis or golf, I'd go nuts."

Diane pursued a degree in merchandising at Endicott College and worked summers at Saks Fifth Avenue in Chicago, both in merchandising and as a model. During one workday, a man tapped her on the shoulder and introduced himself as her birth father, a man she had not seen since she was four years old. The meeting was brief. He told her he had cashed in a life insurance policy, handed her the check and walked away. She never saw him again.

The Alfred Halle & Sons meat market in Berlin, New Hampshire, 1910. The market was founded by Bruce Halle's great-grandfather, Alfred Antoine Halle, in 1904.

Bruce Halle's first grade class at St. Kieran's Elementary School, 1936.

Christmas at the McKelvey home, Berlin, New Hampshire, 1937. Top to bottom: Fred Sr., Molly, Fred Jr., Bruce, Bob, Jim and Alan.

From left to right: Alan, Jim, Bob, Bruce and Fred Jr. at Akers Pond, New Hampshire.

The Halle family in Detroit, 1944. Top row: Betty Lou, Molly, Fred, Mary Ellen and Bruce. Bottom Row: Alan, Bob and Jim.

Bruce at Holy Redeemer football practice, mid-1940s.

Graduation from Holy Redeemer High School, Detroit, 1948.

Fred Jr., Bob and Bruce hoist Fred Halle Sr. while on leave in 1950.

Bruce Halle and Geraldine Konfara at their wedding, March 1951.

On the Armistice line in Korea, 1952.

Halle sold cars to support himself and his family while finishing his college studies.

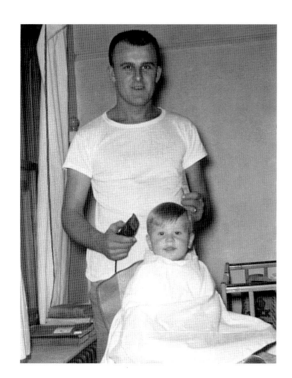

Bruce with Bruce Jr. at home in Belleville, Michigan, 1955.

Bruce at the failing Automotive Supply Company, 1959.

The first Discount Tire store opened January 1960 in Ann Arbor, Michigan, and continued operating at this location until 1989, when the shop moved to a larger building.

As offered in this 1964 advertisement, Halle would give customers the shirt off his back—and then some—to make a sale.

Discount Tire introduced the Arizonian tire after California tire retailer Sam Winston began marketing the Californian. Due to freight costs in the early years, the company sold few Arizonian tires in Arizona.

As the company grew, Discount Tire upgraded and standardized its store designs to look brighter and cleaner than customers might expect.

Store interiors are painted white, have minimal clutter and are cleaner than most customers expect from an automotive supply store. Store bathrooms often feature grooming aids and other amenities to make a positive impression on customers.

Bruce, Gerry and Bruce Jr. at the company's 25th anniversary celebration in 1985. At the end of that year, the company had 140 stores and $161 million in revenue.

Bruce and Gerry (pictured here in Aspen, Colorado) developed a love of skiing in Michigan and continued to pursue the sport after their move to Arizona.

In much of California, stores operate under the name America's Tire. The alternate store name was developed in response to potential confusion with another retailer whose name includes the word "discount."

When Barcelona hosted the 1992 Olympics, Discount Tire's Tahoe party took on an Olympic theme that included Halle's entrance in a tracksuit.

Halle greets the crowd at the company's 1994 celebration at the Biltmore Hotel in Phoenix, Arizona. He made his entrance to the party on a motorcycle.

Diane Cummings and Bruce Halle were married in 1995 after a whirlwind romance.

Since 1996 was an election year, Bruce and Bruce Jr. welcomed their team with a whistle-stop style speech in Lake Tahoe.

Halle presents the American Academy of Achievement's Captain of Achievement award to his friend, Francois Michelin, chair of Michelin Group, 1997.

Daughters Susan and Lisa with Bruce at the 500th store celebration, 2002.

In 2005, Discount Tire's 10-second "Old Lady Ad" was recognized by the Guinness Book of World Records as the longest-running ad in television history. The ad continues to be shown daily in regions where Discount Tire stores are located.

Bruce and Diane Halle at their investiture as Knight Commander and Dame Commander of the Pontifical Order of St. Gregory the Great at the Vatican, 2006.

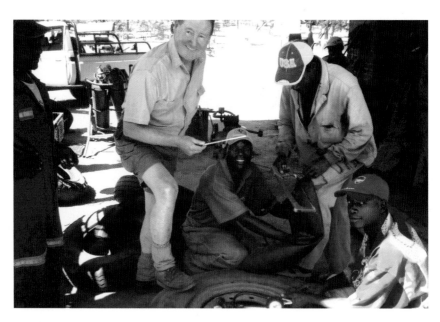

When Halle's cousin, Tim McKelvey, experienced flat tires in Zimbabwe in 2008, he was delighted to find that the rancher who offered to repair his tires had a Discount Tire pressure gauge. Halle described the find as proof that DTC is "an international conglomerate."

Halle mixes it up with the Chenille Sisters at the 2008 corporate party at the Broadmoor Hotel. (Photo by Paul Sharp)

Bruce, Diane and their extended family in 2008. (Photo by Paul Markow)

Halle (center) meets at Discount Tire headquarters with (from left) construction chief Dan Wainwright, chief counsel Jim Silhasek, CEO Tom Englert, strategy chief Michael Zuieback and vice chair Gary Van Brunt. (Photo by Paul Markow)

Halle congratulates new store manager Erik Dodier at the opening of store 798, an America's Tire store in Fontana, California. From left: regional vice president Todd Richard, Dodier, Fontana Mayor Pro Tem John Roberts, Halle and vice chair Gary Van Brunt. (Photo Courtesy of Kori Cruz Photography)

Continuing the heritage and example of her grandmother, Diane became a committed Catholic. Eddie Meyers was Jewish, however, and the family's social sphere began to gravitate toward successful Jewish families. In 1963, while Bruce Halle was establishing his partnership with Ted Von Voigtlander and considering a second store, Diane Meyers married Ivan Zuieback, whose father had founded a successful chain of women's clothing stores in Detroit. She moved with Ivan to the Motor City, where she kept house and managed a career as a model for car advertisements.

At about the time Bruce Halle was opening his third store less than sixty miles away in Flint, Michigan, Diane gave birth to her only child, Michael, in 1966. Three years later, as Bruce and Gerry were relocating to Arizona, the Zuiebacks were divorced, and Diane moved back to Chicago with her son.

Back in Chicago, Diane met Herb Cummings, a widower and father of three grown children. Like Ivan Zuieback, Herbert Cummings was Jewish. His father, Nate, had founded Sara Lee Corporation. Diane and Herb married in 1973, with a rabbi officiating, and renewed their vows fifteen years later with a priest.

Herb and Diane moved to Paradise Valley in 1980 and committed themselves to philanthropy in their newly adopted state. Diane became a trustee of the Phoenix Art Museum and Scottsdale Center for the Arts and, later, joined the New York–based Nathan Cummings Foundation, established in memory of Herb's father.

Philanthropy and civic boards were new territory for Diane, but she considered it a major educational opportunity. As she became more deeply involved with the Phoenix Art Museum, art appreciation turned into a passion, and her board commitment became a nearly full-time occupation.

She and Herb were sought out by charities and other institutions. Black-tie events seemed to be a weekly occurrence. While Herb preferred that his wife not hold a paying job, Diane was applying the work ethic instilled in her by Eddie Meyers to build the success of her adopted institutions. By all visible standards of measurement, Diane Cummings was leading the life her mother had wished for her back in Chicago.

That life came to an end in April, 1992, when Herb Cummings succumbed to pancreatic cancer. As had been the case for Bruce when Gerry was diagnosed with cancer, the year of Herb's illness and his eventual death sent Diane into a tailspin. Following the example set by her grandmother, Diane set one year as the appropriate mourning period and stayed to herself for most of that time.

As Bruce had done since Gerry's passing in 1989, Diane sought the counsel of Father Ray Bucher, who had headed The Casa, the Franciscan Renewal Center in Paradise Valley, Arizona. Bruce's and Diane's lives were already intertwined on several levels through their involvement in the church and with Father Ray.

Father Ray was on a sabbatical when Herb died. When he returned to Phoenix at the start of 1993, Diane was on the board of The Casa and put together a party for him at her home—her first social event since Herb's passing. Father Ray invited Bruce Halle, who attended the party with a woman he was dating at the time. It was the first time Bruce and Diane would be formally introduced.

Soon after the dinner, Bruce asked Diane out, but she declined. She had not completed her one-year mourning period. Her first venture back into black-tie society would come with the 1993 Crisis Nursery gala. Having recovered from his bike accident, Bruce Halle was attending with his daughter, Susan. Diane Cummings attended with friends.

Several months later, after morning Mass, Bruce approached Diane again and invited her to have coffee with him. She was heading to a meeting with directors of the Phoenix Art Museum, however, and turned him down a second time.

A few weeks later, as president of the Phoenix Art Museum, she visited Halle with a mandate from her board to obtain a donation from "that cheap SOB." In fact, he had not been approached prior to that time. The two met for lunch in Carefree, Arizona, north of Scottsdale, and Halle came up with a $10,000 pledge.

As the months passed, Father Ray kept in touch with both Bruce and Diane, enlightening them with news of each other's progress. Halle had asked Mrs. Cummings out twice, though, and had met with her as a donor once. He wasn't quite ready to ask a third time.

When the Phoenix Art Museum wanted Halle to renew his gift in June 1994, he refused to meet with anyone other than Diane. She selected a decidedly unromantic locale for the meeting: the Hearty Hen restaurant, a barbecue joint.

"So I had to go out again and have lunch with him," Diane recalls. "He gave me the $10,000 in the first two seconds and asked me if there was anything else he could do. I said he could bus inner-city children to the museum, and he asked how much that would be. I said $100,000, and he said he'd think about it."

Halle came up with the additional $100,000, but he was thinking about more than donations. Five years after Gerry's death, Bruce Halle was tired of being alone, he was ready to get serious, and he was very attracted to Diane Cummings. As Bruce escorted Diane back to her car, he asked her out for a third time. She said yes, but both of them were going to be traveling over the next few weeks, and Diane was heading up to her home in Jackson Hole, Wyoming.

The two made a date to meet in Phoenix for dinner, but Halle decided to cut the waiting time by flying up to Jackson Hole. With no hotels available, Diane invited him to stay at the house with her and her mother. Halle arrived in time for dinner and spent the night talking with Diane and her mother and, later, dancing on the patio with Diane.

Bruce Halle had never been on Diane's radar in Arizona, though both were donors to some of the same institutions. Now, hosting him at her Wyoming retreat, she found him to be an entertaining conversation partner and a good storyteller. Likewise, Halle found her to be intelligent and easy to talk to, and he thought of her as a morally upright individual he could respect. Equally important, she was widowed, not divorced, which was important to Halle.

Halle decided to enhance any positive impression he was making by inviting Diane to have lunch the next day at a restaurant he liked.

Postrio.

In San Francisco.

Halle had learned the value of incentive flights when he sent three of his executives to California for dinner in 1979, and the flight to San Francisco had a similar effect on Diane Cummings.

The next day, Diane's mother received two dozen white lilies from Bruce, but no flowers arrived for Diane. The reason, she learned, was that "he heard I only like white roses, and there weren't enough white roses in Jackson Hole. So they were flying them in, and I would get them later that afternoon."

Now that the ice had been broken in a big way, Bruce took firm control of the situation. He and Diane quickly became a couple, and Bruce was anxious to close the deal.

"I think it was our sixth date, and he invited me to come out to Aspen," Diane relates. "We were up there about two days and he said, 'We're going to fly to San Diego.' I said, 'We are? I didn't pack to go to San Diego.' He said, 'Not a problem. I want you to meet my children. We'll stay at my daughter Lisa's house.' I said, 'Please, please let's stay at a hotel. I beg you, please.' He said, 'It's not a problem. We'll just go there.'

"Lisa wasn't married, didn't have children and I felt so sorry for her, I was devastated for her," Diane says. "She put me in a downstairs guest bedroom. She put Bruce upstairs in a bedroom next to her."

Susan Halle, Bruce's older daughter, lived about a mile away from Lisa's home and had just returned from exercise class, in her leotard, sweating, when the doorbell rang the next day.

"She opens the door and says, 'Dad, it's so good to see you,'" Diane relates. "Then he said, 'I brought a friend of mine I want you to meet, Diane Cummings.' Susan just says, 'Ah, come on in. Would you like iced tea?' They didn't know what to do with me."

Beyond their difference in backgrounds, the speed of the courtship took family and friends by surprise.

"When Gerry died it was a huge, huge blow to Bruce," recalls Shel Diller, Halle's longtime friend and business associate. "He suffered in silence, although we knew he was really, really hurting. He went off to Aspen a lot and brooded a bit and, being Jewish like I am, I felt I had to fix him up, but he wasn't interested in any of them.

"One day, I'm at our home in La Quinta and the telephone rings, and it's Bruce. He says, 'I want you to meet someone.' So he flew over with this woman who knocked our socks off. It was Diane."

Shel and Marty Diller went to Morton's restaurant with Bruce and Diane that evening, and Bruce announced that they would be getting married. It was October, just four months after their first date in Jackson Hole.

Diane was concerned about the response from Bruce's children, but he told her the children had no vote. He hadn't told his children whom to marry, and he wasn't going to ask them to make the decision for him. Still, when Bruce and Diane called Michael to announce their plans, Bruce came on the line first to ask Michael's permission.

Michael Zuieback was absolutely not a lost boy like Bruce Halle and the men who'd helped him build the country's largest tire chain. With an MBA from Thunderbird and a management position at Johnson Controls in Milwaukee, Zuieback was targeting a career that included larger corporations and global business opportunities. Tire retailing, and Discount Tire in particular, were nowhere on his radar. Roughly five years later, he would join Discount Tire as its first corporate strategy chief.

With the engagement announcements completed, Bruce and Diane considered the terms of their prenuptial agreement. With both entering the marriage with substantial assets, each was prepared to put some terms on paper.

"We went down to the K Club down in the Caribbean, and we took all of three hours to get it done," Diane recalls. "That is when I first realized that I was really going to be a partner, because he had a great partnership with Gerry, and then he said, 'I can do that again.'"

Bruce T. Halle and Diane Meyers Cummings were married on February 11, 1995, at St. Mary's Basilica in Phoenix. Bruce had taken little care of his own home since Gerry had died, so the couple decided to live in Diane's home. It was a major adjustment.

"Bruce moved into my house with his dog, Bo. I was very fastidious about my house, and the dog terrified my staff," Diane says. "So, how did Bruce solve the problem? He thought about it for twenty seconds and went out and bought me this cute little dog that we still have today.

Everybody just melted over this little dog. So, Bruce's dog stayed, and our new dog stayed, and everybody in the household was happy. He solved the problem."

Of course, he hadn't solved all of the problem, because Bo was not quite as fastidious as his new mistress. "His dog chewed up seven sofas," Diane says. "Bruce didn't care. But when the dog chewed up the seventh sofa, I had had it, so I invisible-fenced all the rooms that had sofas. That time, I found the solution."

Bruce and Diane's children, all adults, adapted quickly to the new family dynamic. Michael and Sheila Zuieback became fast friends with Lisa and Chris Pedersen, and the two couples began traveling together with their children. Sheila Zuieback introduced Bruce Jr. to her friend, Nikki, who married Bruce Jr. in 2005.

"Diane really does a good job with the family," Bruce says. "She talks to Susan and Sheila and Nikki and Lisa. She talks to all the girls on a regular basis. And, of course, because of her planning and her foresight, we can take the kids and the grandkids on family trips."

As Diane Halle settled into her new life with the tire king of Arizona, she considered some of the ways she could design a shared life for the two of them as a couple. Each brought ample experience to their marriage, but she was determined to find something new that would be theirs alone.

THE WORLD ACCORDING TO BRUCE

Shortly after Bruce Halle and his family moved to Arizona in 1969, the family was heading home from an evening out in Scottsdale. Gerry remembered that they were out of milk, and the nearest convenience store was about eight miles up Scottsdale Road.

Halle decided to make a run for it on the dark boulevard. With no stoplights between him and the nearest Circle K store, he just might make it before the store closed for the night. Racing north at twice the speed limit, Halle saw a set of flashing lights in his rearview mirror. As the constable gave chase, Halle rolled down his window and waved his arm in a circular motion, which the cop interpreted, correctly, to mean "follow me."

Halle pulled into the parking lot of the Circle K with the police car close behind. The cop jumped out to ask Halle about his emergency.

"I said, 'There's no emergency,'" Halle relates, "'but I just needed to get here before they closed and I figured you were going to give me a ticket anyway, so at least I'd get the milk.' And he said, 'You're right. I am going to give you a ticket.' And he did.

"He was a really nice guy."

Bruce Halle finishes stories and descriptions with "He was a nice guy" the way other people punctuate their statements with "ya know." Sometimes he says *nice guy*, and other times a person was *cool* or *a neat lady*. Whichever word he chooses, though, Halle makes it clear that he finds something to like in everyone.

As a boy in Berlin, New Hampshire, Halle learned to be grateful for the bounty he received from friends and family. The men at the firehouse made skis and a springboard for the Halle boys. Grandpa McKelvey took the Halles into his home. In turn, Molly and Fred shared what they had with their neighbors. Bruce Halle began to internalize the connections of the community and the dependence of each person on everyone else. He couldn't explain it at the time, but it became part of his understanding of how the world around him worked.

The lessons were all deceptively simple, the kind that people pay lip service to but do not follow as resolutely as common sense dictates. "Do unto others . . ."; "It is better to give than to receive"; "Cast your bread upon the waters . . ."; "As we forgive those who trespass against us . . ." The basics of Catholic teaching and parental guidance had been etched permanently in Bruce Halle's mind.

One of the most important lessons he learned was gratitude—a true appreciation of each kindness received. When Ray Walk loaned him the money to pay for his wedding, "I thought that was terrific." When a farmer picked up a hitchhiking Halle on a tractor and then switched to a truck to get him to his wedding faster, "I'll always remember him. That was super." Bill DiDonato, who took Halle's investment and, along with Halle, lost it all in just a few years, was "one of the nicest guys you'll ever meet."

In the years after his family left Berlin, Halle would be rewarded by many people and disappointed by others. When a store manager or other contact would steal from him, the negative experience wouldn't change his hopes and trust for the next person he met. Bruce Halle gives everyone he meets the benefit of the doubt, which leads most people to work hard to justify his trust. There was no calculus to his willingness to trust everyone; it was simply a variation of the Golden Rule.

Halle would receive praise for his own kindnesses, but he learned early to recognize and note those traits in others, not himself. In the close-knit community of Halles, McKelveys and their neighbors, he learned the responsibility each person has to support his extended family. From the punishments he earned by climbing Mount Forist with his brothers, he learned to take his punishment and move on—strictly business.

The world according to Bruce is one in which negative thoughts are a waste of time, he is still the rough-edged guy who couldn't sell insurance, and tires are pretty much irrelevant to the success of Discount Tire.

If pride goeth before a fall, Bruce Thomas Halle is determined to stay on two feet. Although he is clearly and unabashedly happy with his success, he takes pains to deflect most of the praise that people send his way and quickly notes the multitude of mentors and supporters who have played critical roles in his rise. He sees himself as hardworking, but also lucky, as both a reverent man and a sinner. Most likely, he is measurably holier than thou, but he will be the last person to suggest that possibility.

In fact, Halle's greatest discipline might not be the development of tire stores but a passion for humility. Arriving in Arizona in 1969, buying a comparatively large home, adding horses to the nuclear family, vacationing in Aspen and buying jets could add a bit of arrogance to most personalities. Halle found the balance, almost always, by seeing himself as lucky, and possibly a little bit blessed, but never chosen.

"Bruce is the most completely integrated human being I know," says Lattie F. Coor, Ph.D., past president of Arizona State University and the University of Vermont and now chairman and CEO of the Center for the Future of Arizona. "Who he is and how he expresses it, what he does with it, is absolutely a manifestation of someone who knows who he is, knows what he wants, knows what he wants to do, and doesn't need to show off.

"Bruce and his company are one. His philosophy is focused—not exclusively, but focused—on what is good for his people in his company. He demonstrates that you can live a successful life without abandoning your personal beliefs or stretching or altering what you do or who you are.

You can also be immensely successful without lording it over other people, being obnoxious about it."

Halle describes himself in somewhat less glowing terms, always as a work in progress and as flawed as any other human being. His self-image is anchored—possibly marooned—in a small, underfunded and understocked store in Ann Arbor, Michigan. Or perhaps he is still walking along the railroad tracks, carrying his dad's lunch pail to the firehouse from the house his family shares with his grandparents.

"I think of myself as an ordinary guy who goes to work every day and has been lucky enough to live as long as I have, and I have been blessed to have beautiful people around me," Halle reflects. "People sometimes say, 'Gee, how did you do what you do? How did you build the company?' Well, I worked at it for fifty years. You go back and what do you do? You do the things that anybody did when they started a business. You sweep the floors. You wash the windows. You clean the bathrooms. You talk to all the customers. You create some little advertising programs. You pay the rent and try and make it work, and little by little, all the pieces kind of come together."

Diane Halle says it would be a mistake to think that Bruce is ambivalent about the success he's achieved. "He doesn't want to brag about it, but he's happy inside. He's happy where he is today, he was happy where he was ten years ago, and he'll be happy where he could be ten years from now," she declares. "He does love climbing that ladder, but it's the challenge of climbing, to get to that next place, and it doesn't matter if it's in business or if it's in real estate buying or in learning about art or traveling or better clothes or new airplanes. Anything. He likes to learn all about it."

Acquiring and learning have elevated Halle's lifestyle, but not his attitude. Over the years, Halle has developed both an appreciation for and some expertise in oenology, but the lover of fine wine has avoided the temptation, if he had any, to become a wine snob. Ask him for his opinion about wine and he will offer a simple deflection: "The best wine," says Bruce, "is the one I'm drinking now."

Despite all the pieces that have come together for Halle, he doesn't see himself on the same level as other successful businesspeople or professionals.

"Anybody can open tire stores. Lots of people. And what's so wonderful about that?" Halle asks. "I look at people like Warren Buffet, and then I look at some of the big money people and how they do things. It's a whole different world. It's a finance world that I live in, somewhat, because of our size. But my real finance guys are [CFO] Christian [Roe] and [Assistant Treasurer] Andrew [Haus] and those guys. I don't live in the finance world like major developers or mergers and acquisition people do. That's not my dance. And I'm not a doctor. I'm not a dentist. I'm not a college professor— I open tire stores."

Halle continues to place himself in a sphere below the "polished" people who have always seemed to be a bit beyond his reach. "I immediately respected them," he says of countless elegant folks he's met. "They were charming, polished. They had vocabularies. They spoke well. They presented themselves well, and I just kind of admired them. In my opinion, that was something I did not have and I respected it, I admired it."

Entering the world of polished people has always required a passport for Halle, and he has seen the women in his life as the holders of that passport. Both Gerry and, later, Diane have played the role of guide to society. Ask about the most embarrassing moment in Halle's life and his answer will not involve business or personal dealings, but a fashion faux pas.

"We had moved to Arizona and Gerry was at the beauty shop, and she met another lady whose husband was a doctor in town. He was a plastic surgeon, and he belonged to a food and wine organization, Bacchus," Halle recalls. "They met once or twice a year to have a black-tie dinner and taste great wines—just men. So he invites me to go to this. I don't have a tuxedo at that time, so I go to one of the stores in town to get one. It's summertime in Arizona and some gentleman is telling me I should have a white jacket, so I do it. Then I go there and there's twenty-five or thirty guys, and I'm the only one with a white jacket. *That* was embarrassing."

While Halle is still awed by the elegant people of the world, he reserves his respect for those who work hard to accomplish something in life, the "squared away" people who are "honest and straightforward." He admires Karl Eller less for his financial success than for his determination to pull himself back up after hitting bottom with Circle K. He respects his brother, Bob, for building a successful career as an educator and, along with his wife, Nancy, raising a good family. He is proud of his sister, Mary Ellen, for her success building homes with her husband, Roger. He cites Gerry and former Goodyear executive Bill Sweatt as models to be followed in speaking positively about others.

Halle's list of respected individuals is populated by people who work hard, do the right thing and help others. Delving into his disrespected list takes substantial prodding, as he'd rather not talk about the disappointments in life.

"Something that most people say at one time or another—and some more frequently, especially if they go to church regularly—is the Lord's Prayer. And, part of the Lord's Prayer is 'forgive us our trespasses as we forgive those who trespass against us.' People forget that second part. They say it and they don't think about it. It's just words."

But Halle thinks about the second part of that prayer frequently, and he views the forgiveness of others, in large part, as a prerequisite to being forgiven himself.

"I think I'm a positive thinker. I do. I don't dwell on negative things. Some things happen that I don't like once in a while, but it doesn't matter that much," Halle suggests. "I imagine I could think of a couple of shitheads if I spent some more time on it, but it's just not that important. And you don't hear our guys talking negatively about people. Why do that? That's not their M.O. That's not how they live. We look at the positive things and what we can do to make things better and make the company grow, help our people. These are all the things that are important. I'll have to spend some time and think about this. If I come up with the names of a couple of shitheads, I'll tell you."

Of course, no list of shitheads follows the interview, and Halle stresses the need for everyone, including himself, to hold to the basics of honesty and fair dealing.

"Whenever you do something that you shouldn't do, or fail to do something that you should do, you're always the first to know, but don't be surprised when the rest of the world finds out about it," he explains to anyone who will listen to this mantra. Halle's focus on Golden Rule basics is deceptively simple. Everyone knows it, anyone can follow it, but making it a consistent discipline is hard work.

"You cannot tell someone you're a good guy," Halle says simply. "You just have to be one."

Father Ray Bucher says Halle does an unusually good job of walking the walk. "I don't know if he saw it in his folks or he developed it himself," Bucher observes. "But there is an underlying integrity that gets him through storms and high points and low points. I think his faith is a part of it. He knows humans are imperfect and he accepts that."

In fact, Bruce Thomas Halle is probably more polished than he realizes, or will allow himself to accept, in his ninth decade of life. His discipline of humility helps him bridge the gap with his workers and make them feel appreciated. In fact, it is hard to know if it is a discipline at this point, or whether he has somehow hardwired it into his nervous system.

In turn, Halle's employees respond to him with an unusual mixture of familiarity and awe. Most call him Mr. Halle, as a sign of respect, but they also see him as a peer or, sometimes, a father figure. In turn, Halle's uncertainty around the "polished gentlemen" he's met in society is nonexistent when he's hanging with the men in the stores.

Halle seldom talks about business, preferring to talk to individuals about their lives, families and interests. More comfortable in a one-on-one discussion than he is on a stage, Halle sees his success as tied to the success of each individual within the organization.

"The first thing I was told as an employee, and the first thing I ask my guys, is, 'What would Bruce do?'" says Ron Archer, vice president for the

Indiana region. "Once, I saw him in Houston, and he was heading back to Arizona, so he gave me a ride on the corporate jet. For two and a half hours on the ride back, we never talked about business at all. He said he just wanted to get to know his people better, know about their families, so we didn't talk about market share or any business at all. It felt like a couple of guys sitting on a bar stool, shooting the breeze."

In a very meaningful way, there has been essentially no change in Halle's worldview or value system since he was a twelve-year-old boy climbing on board the train that would take him from Berlin to Detroit. The lessons are deceptively simple; obvious but difficult to implement.

1. Be honest.

2. Work hard.

3. Have fun.

4. Be grateful.

5. Pay forward.

It was only half as many lessons as the Decalogue, but Halle found a way to establish both a business empire and thousands of loyal followers by adhering to a handful of the precepts that everyone knows to be true.

I'M CHECKING HIS PROGRESS

In the nearly six years between Gerry's death and the wedding of Bruce and Diane, Discount Tire continued its aggressive growth. By the time the nation's largest tire entrepreneur remarried, he and his lost boys had added more than seventy stores and four regions to the Discount Tire empire.

While Diane focused on uniting the families and consolidating households, Bruce presented his own to-do list for his new bride. Gerry had been the Discount Tire Mom since the beginning in Ann Arbor. Now it was Diane's turn to fill that role. The mantle of "founder's wife" turned out to be more than a full-time job in a company whose founder was personally acquainted with thousands of employees and spouses.

As she became more deeply involved in the Bruce Halle family, including the extended network of Discount Tire employees, Diane reduced or eliminated her ties to many of the civic endeavors that had defined her role as the wife of Herb Cummings. Art and philanthropy continued to be passions, however, and she focused on these areas to create a shared journey for Mr. and Mrs. Bruce Thomas Halle.

Both had developed a keen appreciation for Catholic teachings about charity, although the two had taken very different paths in their application of those lessons. Diane focused on philanthropy, which seeks to address broad issues or common needs, working from the top down to create a better world. Bruce had more of a retail approach, opening his wallet to individuals with a sad story or an immediate hardship.

As a result, Halle's personal files are filled with letters from employees, family, friends and quite a few strangers who came up short and called on him for help. Attached to those letters, quite often, are copies of the checks he has sent in response. Across the company, just about every manager can cite a case of an employee or family member whose crisis was resolved by Bruce Halle. The prototypical statement, repeated across the company and across the decades, follows a simple pattern: "My relative/ friend/employee had a disaster/illness and Bruce Halle provided a check/ referral/flight/time off." Or all of the above.

A retailer to the core, Halle considered donations on a person-by-person basis, much the same way he thought about selling tires—one at a time. Halle looked after his parents and sent gifts to relatives; supported Father Francis Curran, his parish priest from St. Kieran's in Berlin; and adopted the Little Sisters of the Poor, whose leader had stopped by a store many years earlier with a battered vehicle and dangerously worn tires. Examples offered by employees—seldom mentioned by Halle himself— number in the thousands.

Each of these acts of charity was specific and tangible to Halle, while larger-scale, philanthropic donations were less fulfilling, even if the importance of the cause was clear.

Halle also was concerned about the publicity that surrounded large donations and highlighted his wealth. While employees know Halle has achieved great wealth, he sees no reason to stand in a spotlight and give money that could go toward the employees' families to other causes.

"We had a luncheon a few years ago with the president of a university, and he was looking for a big funding program in line with a $40 million to $50 million gift the university had received earlier," Halle remembers.

"So he took Diane and me to lunch, and we knew he was going to ask for something. So he finally gets through the nice luncheon and all the nice talking and he finally gets to a number. He says he wants $35 million from me. He's saying the publicity is good for us and so on, but that's the last thing I want. If I'm going to give $35 million to anybody, I'm going to give it to my employees and their families.

"It would be terrible for me to give big money, like millions of dollars, to someplace and get all that publicity out of it. And here I've got employees out there who are ordinary working people, making a good living, but nothing like that. And all of a sudden I'm giving millions and millions of dollars away. It's stupid. It would be a morale disaster for all of my employees," Halle concludes.

Halle will talk at length about the college scholarships available to children of full-time employees with at least three years on the job, about the "Baby Brain Boxes" the company sends to employees with a new baby and the support employees give to each other through their own fundraising activities. He is less focused on giving outside the universe of his extended family at Discount Tire.

Halle had made a few exceptions, most notably when he agreed to fund the Halle Heart Center in Tempe, Arizona, in memory of Gerry, and a new library at his alma mater, Eastern Michigan University. After Bruce married Diane, the number of these named gifts increased, largely focused on education and health—including cancer—in Arizona.

Diane was anxious to apply the lessons she had learned at the Nate Cummings Foundation to add impact and efficiency to her new husband's generosity. In 2002, the couple established the Bruce T. Halle Family Foundation, with Diane as president, creating a vehicle to expand giving to both public institutions and employee families.

Across the Discount Tire network, employees are following the founder's lead by raising money for all types of causes. Each region has its own employee assistance fund to help employees with unusual medical or other expenses, while Halle makes an additional donation to each of the twenty-three regional offices for gifts to Cub Scouts, Little League teams and other local groups. From the Administrative Angels at corporate headquarters to the wives who put together bake sales for individual stores, the sun never sets on Discount Tire fundraisers.

While local engagement in fundraising builds esprit de corps, funneling donations through regional offices has its limitations. Diane discovered that the vice presidents and assistant vice presidents in the regions were too busy running their operations to give away the money available to them, so she organized their wives to handle the job.

"It really is a big deal, and the wives love it," Diane Halle says. "You hear the stories of site visits that they make—they've taped some of this—and you cry a little. You almost cry listening to it. It's beautiful. The husbands are happy that the wives are doing it, and the husbands, by the way, if they want to sponsor a Little League team, they can still do that. Or they can give a set of tires to a charity. But the women are out there giving money to actual charities."

Diane says the involvement of the wives has made a substantial difference both for the charities and for the wives themselves. Under the umbrella of Driven To Care, the regional wives meet regularly with each other and, at least annually, with Diane Halle to plan activities. The same methods are applied to build spouse involvement at the corporate level, where Diane works with executive wives through Bridges To Hope.

The foundation also manages Discount Tire's scholarship program and other corporate giving, while a multimillion-dollar grant from the Halles supports philanthropy for public causes related primarily to education, health and issues of children and families. Mirroring the corporate-community approach entrenched at Discount Tire, the foundation makes its website available as a resource to both other nonprofits and grant applicants.

Diane sees the family foundation as a means of passing on a commitment to charity to the next generations of the Halle family. By engaging children and grandchildren with the foundation, she hopes to create both momentum and continuity for philanthropic engagement.

Sir Tom Farmer, a longtime friend of Bruce Halle and founder of Quik-Fit Holdings, says it's important for wealthy families to organize their giving in the most productive way.

"Being a Catholic and proper Christian, you aim to have socialist lean-ings in the pure apolitical way. You should try to do things for those less fortunate," Farmer says. "If we're supporting something, we should be clear how much and how long, and we must be able to evaluate it. I think that's what Diane brought to Bruce's giving, a more professional and more con-trolled focus, and more thinking about what and who is going to benefit. In other words, more of the head being involved and not just the heart."

Diane also drew Bruce out of the office more, increasing his travels to weeks rather than days out of Scottsdale. Bruce had agreed to spend three days on their honeymoon—noting it was one day more than he had with Gerry—but he was, in fact, enjoying the style of touring that Diane pre-sented. It was on one such tour that the Halles began their most meaning-ful act of philanthropy.

"It was our first Christmas alone, and we decided to go to Rome for Christmas," Diane says. "We were just going to take ten days and roam Rome. During that time, John McCaffrey, a friend of Sir Tom, was going to be over there. John organized a private tour of the Vatican for us.

"He told us about this huge project to restore the Pauline Chapel, which is the Pope's private chapel, and he said the people who help restore it will get to use the Pauline Chapel for every wedding or baptism for the rest of their lives or the lives of their family. It goes on in perpetuity and, interestingly enough, we would be knighted into the highest order that the Vatican can give a layperson. We're standing there and having a couple of scotches and a bottle of wine, and we're thinking this is really cool. This is something that we should look into and, before you know it, we said, 'Let's do it.'"

When the time came to visit the Vatican in 2006, the Halles chartered a plane to bring forty couples with them for a week of festivities, touring and the knighting ceremony itself. The entourage included family, friends and employees, almost all of whom had known Bruce or Diane for decades.

Larry Allen, regional vice president in Houston, says he and Halle were having dinner after checking out sites for new stores when Bruce "sud-denly leaned over and said, 'I want you to go to Rome with us in October. We'll be going to the Vatican.'"

The week in Rome was like an extended company party, as well as a vacation, with dinners, receptions and tours available to all the guests. Bruce and Diane arranged buses to take their guests to the ceremony and other programs over several days.

The Pauline Chapel was still being renovated at the time of the ceremony, but the group was given a brief tour. The next day, at the front of St. Peter's Basilica, Pope Benedict XVI addressed the throngs who had assembled and came down to greet a number of visitors, including the Halles.

"How do you stand at the Vatican and know that you are receiving the highest lay order of your religion? You almost cannot grasp it," Diane says. "It's an awesome thing. I had said to Bruce the previous year, 'Two things I'd like to do before I die. I'd like to go to the White House and I'd like to meet the Pope,' and within that year, we had gone to the White House and we had met the Pope. How does that happen?"

While the couple began to fuse their approaches to charitable giving and philanthropy, Diane looked for additional ways to create a life that would be uniquely theirs. Art seemed to be a natural fit, considering Diane's history with art collections and the Phoenix Art Museum. However, Bruce and Gerry had traveled this road, at least partially, during their marriage.

Since early in their marriage, Gerry had foraged for tire memorabilia in antique shops and gift stores, seeking out tire-themed ashtrays and other knickknacks. In 1982, she found a lithograph she thought Bruce might like, an old Pirelli Tire poster. That single gift created the impetus for a decades-long search for other tire posters. Ultimately, the Halle collection would grow to nearly 340 posters and would represent a unique perspective on both advertising and the tire industry.

Bruce's interest in tire posters grew organically, not by plan, much like his love of opera and fine wine. Knowing that Gerry was a fan of opera and loved to listen to records at home, Bruce bought her tickets to a live performance, where he became enamored of the spectacle and the art. Responding to an ad from the J.L. Hudson department store in Detroit, where Gerry worked while he was in college, Halle started buying and, later, collecting fine wines. As with the growth of Discount Tire itself, Halle's passions grew more from circumstance than plan.

Now married to the former president of the Phoenix Art Museum, Bruce Halle was about to embark on another journey of discovery. Not surprisingly, Diane came up with a plan.

"Gerry got me started with posters, and Diane got me into art," Halle says simply.

Diane Halle had no formal training in art history, but she had built her passion for the subject through her involvement with the Cummings family and the Phoenix Art Museum. As a volunteer at the museum, she stopped giving tours and began working in the library as a means to absorb more about her chosen avocation.

Looking for a niche in a well-established profession, Diane began to focus on Latin American art, making a few investments in selected pieces early in her years with Bruce.

"We're in the state of Arizona and, at that time, they said one quarter of the population in a couple of years is going to be Hispanic," she recalls. "I thought Latin American art was the natural progression. It was the time. I was in the right state. So I began."

Diane saw the project on several levels. On the surface, Latin American art represented a largely undiscovered niche. More significant, the journey would be an experience she and Bruce, both well established as adults, could create together. Bruce was game, as he is for most new adventures.

"He's a sponge. He absorbs everything. He's interested to know about things that he's not even interested in," Diane says happily. Diane was interested in Latin American art, so Bruce was interested, too.

Enlisting the guidance of art experts Roland Augustine and Beverly Adams, the newlyweds traveled to Argentina, Brazil, Peru and Ecuador, as well as art festivals and galleries around the world. As was the case with charity, each approached their journey from a slightly different perspective. While Diane began to develop the context for their collection, Bruce tended to focus on individual pieces and, often, the backstory of the artist.

One of the first pieces Diane wanted to buy was a ten-foot square painting with a grid and polka dots on bright orange paper, a painting titled *Rafter: Hell Act II* by Cuban émigré Luis Cruz Azaceta. Toward one corner of the canvas, Azaceta is adrift on a raft, hemmed in by the grid in a sea of orange.

"Not in my house," Bruce declared.

Diane bought the painting and it did, in fact, hang in their house. The next time Azaceta was in Phoenix, Diane arranged a dinner with him at the Halle home and seated him next to Bruce. Bruce and the artist discussed the artist's life in Cuba, his escape from that island nation and his sense of estrangement from his native land.

By the end of the evening, Bruce liked the painter, which made him like the painting of a little man trapped in a sea of orange.

"Every day, I check his progress," he says now.

The Halles developed a simple system for their collection. If both of them like a piece, it hangs in their home in Paradise Valley. If he doesn't like the piece and Diane finds it worth having, it's displayed elsewhere. While Diane sees the Latin American art collection as a legacy to be built and passed on, Bruce is more of the "I know what I like" persuasion.

"I'm buying sculptures, and I only buy things that appeal to me, that I like to look at," Bruce says. "I'm not going to buy it because the artist is famous or popular. I don't care about that. I care about what I look at."

As Diane worked to create a shared journey into philanthropy and art, Bruce introduced her to a way of life and thinking that she had not fully appreciated before meeting him. Most important was his focus on the importance of the individual, a focus that had enabled him to attract and retain loyal followers for more than thirty-five years.

"I have learned to care much more about people who work for me. They have become my family," she says. "They do things for me that are above and beyond the call of duty, and for that I will be forever grateful, and I will show them. That's what Bruce has taught me: how to treat people.

"I've also learned from Bruce not to worry so much. Don't be so nervous about the next moment. Live and enjoy it. And, live life to its fullest. Don't try to micromanage everything. Relax."

Diane begins speaking faster about lessons learned.

"I have a problem and I figure out the solution. I'm set. I know it from beginning to end," she relates. "So I explain it to Bruce, 'This is how I'm going to do it.' Then he looks at me and says, 'So, are you asking me my opinion?' 'Yes, I'd like to hear what you have to say.' He'll take it and make just like two little moves and it's done. He figures out instantly how to put the pieces of the puzzle together in the fewest steps. It's amazing, even if it is pretty annoying at the same time."

Father Ray says the couple benefits from two very different ways of thinking and problem solving. "They have different qualities," he says. "In some ways, I see Bruce as more inductive, very experiential, moving toward the center, and I see Diane as more deductive, applying experiences to long-held principles."

Lattie Coor, founder of the Center for the Future of Arizona and a longtime friend, says both Bruce and Diane changed as they began to build a life together.

"To watch the two of them both grow, and genuinely grow, it's particularly instructive," Coor says. "Bruce Halle hasn't lost an iota of who he is as he's grown into this. He never forgets where he came from, he never forgets who he is, but he's not locked into his world."

PAYING FORWARD

"Take all the guys in your stores, the total number you have, and multiply it by maybe five or six, whatever you want, some number like that, because their families are your responsibility, too," Bruce Halle tells his regional vice presidents on a planning retreat. "As you move up in this company, you just get more and more responsibility, more people depending on you and what you do. It will keep you up at night thinking about it a little bit."

To a great extent, Bruce Halle's family had survived the Depression and the war years because somebody decided his family was their responsibility, too. In most cases, it was the McKelveys, who provided a home in Berlin, a job in Detroit and the ability to buy a home in Taylor Township. Bruce had benefited, individually, from the daily rides provided by Carl Hansen, the confidence of Sister Marie Ellen, the generosity of Ray Walk's loan for his wedding with Gerry and other uncounted kindnesses.

The lesson was clear: good people help others, and those who are helped must pass it on. By the time Bruce Halle graduated from high school, he had developed a focus on taking care of others, from his mother and siblings to the friends he helped to find summer jobs. In college, he scavenged for leftovers at his job in the cafeteria, sharing with fellow students. As a Marine, esprit de corps was drilled into him from day one. As a father and husband, his responsibility to family was irrevocable.

Although Bruce Halle had no leadership role as he left college, his style of servant leadership was already embedded in his DNA. As a company owner, he would see his employees as extended family to be protected. In turn, he would expect those he protected to look out for others.

The mandate to pay it forward is absolute in Halle's mind. Steve Fournier, chief operating officer, remembers the emphatic message he received from Halle when he moved into the corporate office.

"When I was promoted out of the stores, he said to me, 'I bet you're feeling pretty good about yourself, and you'll be going around to all the stores, telling your managers what to do. But just remember that you work for them,'" Fournier says.

Rich Kuipers, senior vice president, says responsibility to others has been etched into the souls of everyone who survives at Discount Tire, while self-importance can be hazardous to one's career.

"Nobody works *for* you. We work *with* people," Kuipers says. "The quickest way to get hammered around here is to think it's about you and not the people you work with."

Halle has no patience for people who achieve success and consider their good fortune to be a reward uniquely deserved. Nobody arrives at his destination without the support of others, no matter what their self-made saga might suggest, and the greatest sin is failing to recognize, acknowledge and repay the favors.

Halle often tells people that he stopped working for money many years ago. As a practical matter, the founder of Discount Tire has more than enough wealth to last several lifetimes. Now, he says, the reason for working is to create new opportunities for the people who are coming up the ranks today.

"All we're doing is creating opportunity and jobs for a lot of wonderful people, just like that was created for you by somebody else," Halle reminds his executives. Halle sees kindness less as something received than as a trust to be passed on to the next person in line. The more kindnesses one receives, the greater the responsibility to pay it forward. As Halle considers the people who run the company today, he looks for that same commitment.

Paul Witherspoon, vice president in Utah, remembers that, "We were traveling on his plane and he said, 'You're responsible for people who aren't even born yet. You're responsible for the kids of employees that haven't been born yet. If we don't create the opportunities for them, we haven't done our job.' And I realized how that applied to me in terms of the opportunity here today for my kids."

Ray Winiecke, vice president of the San Diego region, echoes the belief that the work isn't done until everyone gets to share in the success that Halle created for the current managers.

"It's one thing to say it, but another to actually live it and see it and do it," Winiecke says. "We have the responsibility to make sure the opportunity is available to all our people. We can't bring them in under false pretenses. We can't say there's an opportunity when there isn't. We have to create the opportunity for them like it was offered to us. Our dreams have been realized, but that's not the case yet for everyone around us, so we have to make sure they have the opportunity we had."

The mission to take care of employees includes assistance when families face important challenges. Across the country, employees raise money and make contributions to the Employee Assistance Fund, which provides extra support for families with a sick child or other serious need. While Halle has the capacity to provide that support from his own resources, he sees it as critical for employees to work together to support each other, much as his own extended family did in Berlin and, to a lesser extent, Detroit.

Halle is fond of relating stories about Discount Tire employees who internalized the message about paying forward to others. After sending one employee a check to replace items lost in a fire, Halle received a call from the employee, who said he didn't need all that money but wanted to share it with a neighbor. Halle sent another employee a check for $20,000 to cover medical expenses for the employee's wife, only to receive a refund of the funds he didn't need. Halle remembers dozens of cases of employees winning prizes and giving the money back or sharing it with their workers, and he wants to be sure his executives remember those stories as well.

"I call all employees on their birthdays, which is just a minute but it means a lot," says Todd Richard, Los Angeles vice president. "I used to work for [Houston VP] Larry Allen and he called me on my birthday and it made a difference to me, so I'm doing it now for my employees. We have thirty stores in Los Angeles. Paying it forward now means I have to build as many stores as I can before I retire. I pay it forward by building stores to give my people an opportunity to become store managers and help them become better businessmen, better fathers to their families."

The people who make the connection regarding support for employees also have the mind-set to do the same for the customer. Buying into the "be the dad" culture at Discount Tire almost always entails a recognition of the debt owed to the people who pay the bills.

"We are in the people business, and we just happen to be selling tires," Mark MacGuinness, vice president of Discount Tire Direct, says. "We haven't just adopted this idea as a catchphrase or as part of our vision statement. We live this way. We are truly interested in the happiness of our customers and our people. I train my new hires to take action if they ever meet an unhappy customer. Not just to empathize, but to take action."

Tom Williams, vice president in the Carolinas region, says the relationship of each employee with every individual customer is a direct link to the beginnings of the company, when Halle was opening his first store and greeting his first customer.

"I tell them, 'You are the Mr. Halle of your store and, if you can envision back in those days, it was a matter of survival for him, feeling deep gratitude that they had chosen to buy from him.' We need to treat every customer who comes in our stores today the same way, embrace them as if it was our first customer on our first day."

Richard says the company's practice of giving tires to out-of-luck customers connects each store with the Halle dogma about paying forward. Just as Halle provides benefits or financial support to employees when they are in need, the managers in the stores are called upon to take care of their customers in need.

Greg Smith, vice president in Florida, says the company's practice of giving free tires to poor customers or those whose warranties don't quite cover their specific loss is the most visible example of paying forward to customers.

"It's all about earning the referral, about the word of mouth, and if you have to give away a tire to keep a customer happy, it will come back to you tenfold," Smith says. "We probably give away a tire a week at each store in Florida. A single mom comes in with three screaming kids, four bald tires—one is shot—and it's another week until payday. So we'll loan her a set of tires or just give it to her."

Paying forward is part of the DNA of the people who succeed at Discount Tire, internalized through either genetics or osmosis. Halle is not so much a mentor to his team as he is the prototype to be emulated. Like almost all entrepreneurs, he has a vision to be followed and he is determined to perpetuate that vision throughout the organization.

In his vision, success comes from focusing on what each person owes to his family, to future employees and to the next customer coming in the door. Everyone has an unbreakable contract to pay forward to the next customer, the next employee and the next generation.

It's a simple idea that has driven growth for more than five decades. And Bruce Halle wants to be sure nobody forgets the mission.

PERFECTING THE SYSTEM

"If you go out and spend an extra million dollars on something, how many tires do the guys in the stores have to sell to pay for that?" Bruce Halle asks. "What we have to do is fight bureaucracy, fight it, because it's like a disease that creeps in all by itself."

Halle might love the people who work for him at the corporate office in Scottsdale, but he has a strong belief that oversized corporate staffs can drain the life from an organization by taking too much control from the people in the stores. Worse, every dollar invested at headquarters is a dollar that can't be spent on store expansion.

The company's breakneck pace of store expansion in the 1980s began to expose some cracks in the system, however. Providing the greatest flexibility and independence at the store level can build esprit de corps, but it can also encourage duplication of easily consolidated expenditures, evolution of differing cultures and suboptimal financial performance.

As the 1990s began, CEO Tom Englert recalls, the company had no training department to ensure consistency across the country. Dave Fairbanks and Al Olsen had worked on the company's first training manual in 1981, but not much had been done since then to assure consistency of training and culture.

The company had benefited in the prior decade as a large number of Michiganders moved out to open new regions, bringing the culture and training with them. As the company entered more regions, though, that pattern of migration had become less significant and reinforcement of culture was needed. Similarly, each region and store was reinventing the wheel when it came to advertising and marketing, with no central resource available to buttress the local capabilities.

Across the same period that included the loss of his first wife and his own brush with death, Halle began to acquiesce to expanded corporate functions, but only if they were focused on supporting the stores. He had made a move in that direction in 1986 when he appointed Bruce Halle Jr. to be senior vice president in charge of store operations. In 1990, he brought in Englert in a parallel role, with the mandate to help the regional vice presidents in helping the stores. In 1995, Halle named Bruce Jr. to the role of president and promoted Gary Van Brunt in 1997 to executive vice president—the same role Ted Von Voigtlander had held previously.

Professionally, the awards and recognition continued to grow for the company. In 1998, *Forbes* ranked Discount Tire 281 on its list of the five hundred largest private companies and bumped the company up to 229 in the following year. Industry magazines continued to list the company as the largest independent tire retailer. By the end of the 1990s, Bruce Halle would be atop a network of 416 stores, with 1999 revenue topping $1 billion for the first time.

Von Voigtlander, who had retired from active involvement in the company, died in 1999, but Halle was not allowed to attend the funeral. Although he had continued to provide financial support to his retired partner, Von Voigtlander's widow was not enamored of Bruce Halle. Halle and the widow's attorneys eventually reached agreement on a buyout value for Von Voigtlander's remaining 29 percent of the company, and Halle borrowed the money to pay her off.

The situation still rankles many of the executives who were involved in the transaction, who see Halle's approach as more conciliatory than the situation demanded. Halle concedes that it was a disappointment, but insists he has moved on since then.

Halle named Gary Van Brunt CEO in 1999, making Van Brunt only the second person in nearly forty years to hold that title. In 2000, Halle brought in Diane's son, Michael Zuieback, as an assistant vice president to create a corporate strategy function. Keenly aware of the company's emphasis on promotion from within and bringing executives up through the stores, Zuieback invested substantial time absorbing the culture, simply getting to know the store managers and regional leaders and figuring out what made the company tick.

Soon, he was ready to help the operations team codify and perpetuate the cultural strengths that would sustain the business. While he initiated classic initiatives like strategic planning, he also focused on translating what people already did into the language of a plan. In many ways, the corporate strategy focuses on the culture that creates success, rather than on the dollars that would result from implementation.

Training expanded to focus on the Dream Slide, a visual depiction of all the tools employees would need to utilize in building their careers at Discount Tire. Showing a car being driven toward a store, the slide incorporates messages about personal growth, customer service, financial metrics and teamwork.

While the Dream Slide is a single page of drawings and text, training sessions based on the document can last a day or longer. Running a tire store and building a career at Discount Tire are harder than they might appear on the surface, especially as managers focus on the need to pay forward to both employees and customers.

That focus is emphasized, as well, at the corporate office, where the stores are recognized as the *customers* who need to be delighted by the home office, just as the buying public must be delighted by the stores.

"When we came up with that Dream Slide, people asked, 'Should we have a different slide for the corporate office?'" Lori Governale, vice president of administration, remembers. "I said, 'No, because the company is all about the stores and the customers. When we grow the stores, we create opportunities at the corporate office.'"

Governale says the corporate mission to support the stores can limit the clarity of advancement opportunities for people who are not working in the field. In the stores, growth is applauded, but growing headcounts at corporate is discouraged whenever possible.

"Here, the career path is not as well defined as in the field, because we're a cost center. We're here to support the stores while keeping costs down. We help make it possible for the company to open more stores, and that creates career opportunity at corporate," Governale says. To make sure employees in corporate see their role clearly, the company has begun sending administrative staff on store visits. "The sooner we get them out into the stores to see how things work, the faster they'll understand the Dream Slide and how it relates to their work in the corporate office," Governale says.

Refinements in training have helped the company solidify and focus on the core strengths that grew organically and were transmitted as managers were transferred to new regions in the 1980s. While the company continues to benefit from cross-regional transfers that increase the consistency of acculturation, a company that plans to operate one thousand stores or more needs to standardize its programs.

Halle has never been afraid to experiment with new ideas, but experiments have become more limited and infrequent as Discount Tire grew. The first diversification into general auto service at Dave Fairbanks's Huron Valley Tire store failed, as did the membership-based Tires Plus Club and the diversion into battery sales.

Still willing to experiment, though not under the Discount Tire Name, Halle opened a pair of Network Alignment stores in 1992 in Arizona to provide alignment, brake and other services under a different corporate name. Again, the experiment failed and Halle sold the stores to their managers just three years later.

In 2002, Discount Tire tried a new approach to flat repairs by charging customers upfront and then giving them vouchers to use on a future tire purchase. The voucher program offered no "wow factor" to customers and seemed, in the customers' minds, to be no different from the competitors who charged for repairs all along. Two years later, the company returned to free repairs with no vouchers.

Around the same time, Halle assigned son-in-law Chris Pedersen to create a mobile tire service for people who wanted tires installed at their homes or offices. Pedersen ran the service for a few years, but that business never gained traction, either.

In all these diversifications, the company found it impossible to replicate the success Halle had found in simply replacing tires. Discount Tire, it turns out, had developed a hedgehog concept in 1960, but required more than four decades to determine that they could not improve on the model. (A hedgehog concept, of course, is the idea posited by Jim Collins in *Good to Great* that the best companies find one thing they can do better than anyone and focus on that one thing.)

In the end, Halle's hedgehog was not selling tires but motivating employees to provide better customer service than peers. In a commodity business, that has proven to be enough to drive the company from a single store to the top of its industry.

THE BUMBLEBEE

As Discount Tire gained traction as one of the nation's largest independent tire retailers, skepticism about its business model faded into grudg-
ing respect and, ultimately, admiration. It didn't take long before potential
buyers, investment bankers and other investors started sniffing around,
suggesting to Halle that he sell the company or go public. Several of his
primary competitors took the bait, but Halle has been adamant in his
refusal to engage in any discussions on the subject.

"We are approached and we won't even talk about it, because if we
talk about it, it will start rumors, and we're not going to sell it," Halle says.
"These capital people, with all the money they have to spend, they want to
buy everything, but you know what they do to companies. They rape and
pillage. They really do. It's terrible what they do, so it's not on the agenda.
I won't even talk about that."

Discount Tire would deliver a track record of performance that few
companies could match. Over more than fifty years of operations, the tire
retailer has never had a down year for sales and has never had a layoff. In
2011, Discount Tire recorded more than $3 billion in revenue and ended
the year with more than 820 locations.

While that performance is rare for any company—even surviving fifty years in business is a major achievement—the company's path to success has been rarer still. Discount Tire is a bumblebee, accomplishing what appears on the surface to be impossible. While common wisdom suggests that a bumblebee's short wingspan and rotund torso should preclude flight, bees are not terribly susceptible to the wisdom of the crowd. Similarly, Discount Tire thrives while overpaying its people, keeping employees on the payroll in spite of screwing up, giving away too much product and staying closed when competitors are open for business.

Managers at the company's eight hundred retail stores start with a base salary in the $55,000 to $70,000 range, but bonuses based on store earnings often build their income into six figures. Managers share 10 percent of annual store profits up to the $200,000 level, while their portion of earnings increases to 20 percent when store income surpasses $200,000. In 2011, nearly 60 percent of stores posted earnings over the $200,000 level.

In addition to liberal application of the reset button to salvage the careers of faltering workers, the company will pay bonuses at times to employees who don't meet their profitability goals, especially when the shortfall results from local economic conditions. Halle has approved bonuses in Michigan and other economically challenged areas as a means of keeping employees motivated in difficult markets.

Halle also provides a solid array of employee benefits and frequent gifts for employees as a way of saying thank-you for their commitment. In addition to tuition grants for college, trophies and prizes are awarded to employees' children who are still in elementary school or high school as a means of encouraging their emphasis on education.

"We give a semiannual gift in June or July and another one in December," Halle says. "That's for everybody, and then we have a performance bonus, which does not include everybody, so there are three a year. Why not? Everybody doesn't earn the incentive each year. But every family can always use a few more dollars for whatever they're doing."

Discount Tire's success depends on having the right people on the team, and Halle is willing to make the investment to recruit and retain those people. In a very real sense, Halle pays a price for keeping his stores closed on Sundays, one of the busier days for any retail business, but he wouldn't shortchange his employees on one of the few benefits he allowed himself when he opened his first store.

"He leaves a substantial amount of money on the table in terms of contributions to the 401(k) plan, gifts, bonuses, parties and such," says Jim Silhasek, general counsel. "He could run this place on a really skinny budget and make a lot more profit available to himself personally, but that's not the way he wants to do it."

As a publicly traded company, Discount Tire would get no points for Halle's willingness to approve low-ball budget goals for store managers, either.

"He believes in giving people budgets they can absolutely outperform, which is different from the 'stretch goals' that are more common," CFO Christian Roe says. "He doesn't want people to be disappointed at not reaching their numbers. So we end up with some incredibly positive morale. That's been enormously successful in growing the company over the years."

Halle says he learned the hard way that setting aggressive goals reduces the level of progress by demoralizing people whose markets won't allow success. Setting the bar too high can actually lead to lower performance than setting the bar a bit lower, he says.

"It's wonderful that financial people can sit down and, based on last year's numbers in the market and so on, make some projections as to what we're going to do. That's their job. That's all they do," Halle says. "But they don't make it happen. They're not out there making these projections become true. They've just put them down. In fact, with Christian [Roe] and [Assistant Treasurer] Andrew [Haus], I'll take their projections and I'll cut them by 25 to 30 percent. I've done this. I've cut them heavily. Why? Because here's what happens. Christian is optimistic and comes up with some great numbers. They're all broken down by parts of the country, right down to stores. Sounds wonderful. You're a store manager, and we come up with this overall projection, and it's all broken down, and it's fed from the bottom up to some degree, and we massage it, and we add to it or subtract. Now all of a sudden, you're a store manager, and this whole big, grand thing is done, and we have a projection, and your projection is

X. In the past, our guys had it too high. So, month by month, you can see what you're doing. You're not making X. You're depressed. You're feeling like a failure. You're wondering what's wrong with you and so on and so forth, because X was too high. So my point being to Christian and all my guys, we're going to cut these projections way down. Now, X is X minus something, and all of a sudden, you're meeting it or maybe you're exceeding it. You're happy. You're elated. You're positive. You're pumped up. 'Hey man, I'm successful! I'm doing it.' And you get way above the projection. You feel wonderful. You're a star. You've made money.

"The opposite is a disaster. If you project too high for people, they're a failure all year round. Even though these are projections, by the time they get around the region, to the assistant vice president and to the stores, they're not projections, they're marching orders. That's how they read them."

Halle remembers making the mistake of delivering overly optimistic projections to the stores and watching performance suffer as reality kept the managers from achieving the goals.

"You could sit down and take any store, and come up with a number and say we're going to sell four more tires every day at every store," Halle says. "So, you could take a store and take what they've done in the past, add four tires a day, run the numbers out, and see how much more money they're going to make. It was a mistake on my part because it was an unreasonable goal. You could not do it. So, you're a store manager. You looked at these numbers all the way out. The numbers are truthful. You can't reach them, but they're truthful. There's nobody lying. You see this number and you say, 'I'm going to make this much money. I'm going to get 20 percent of that.' So you go home that night. 'Honey, guess what. I've got these numbers and I'm going to get 20 percent of that.' Your wife says, 'I'm going to get new drapes, a new sofa,' whatever. And everybody is excited, but you don't get there. You can't get there. It's a disaster. I let that happen one year and there were disappointed people all over the country, so we won't make those mistakes again."

Another mistake Halle won't make is overloading his store managers with mandates from the corporate office in Scottsdale. Contrary to general business practice and theory, Discount Tire is built around its employees and the individual store. Stores are treated as independent operating businesses, each with a mission to delight the customer.

Corporate meddling can get in the way of success at the store level and, by transference, the entire company. At corporate headquarters, six executives are responsible for overseeing twenty-three regions. In the regional offices, a total of roughly one hundred vice presidents and assistant vice presidents oversee more than eight hundred stores. The job of management is to hire the right people, immerse them in the corporate culture and get out of the way.

"The guys and gals in the stores run the company," explains Gary LaHaie, senior vice president of purchasing. "It starts all the way down at the neighborhood level in the stores, and then it moves up to the regions, and then corporate. One neighborhood might not be able to afford the same tires as another, and it's up to us to meet the needs of each store."

While the corporate purchasing team works regularly to obtain volume pricing or other breaks from manufacturers, the corporate office won't tell its store managers which tires to push. The company will arrange promotions, but there is no mandate for any store to participate.

"What do we know about what they sell in Lubbock, Texas, or what they should be selling in Lubbock, Texas?" LaHaie asks. "We don't, so we have no business telling them what they should sell. We're not the customer. The people in the stores are serving the customers and driving our company forward, so we need to listen to them."

Halle likens his reliance on individual store managers to the approach Warren Buffett applies in businesses owned by Berkshire Hathaway. It's no more complicated, in his mind, than having the right people working with a profitable business model.

"Warren Buffet has interests in a whole bunch of companies all around the world. He has an interest in them or controls them, or he owns them, whichever. And what Warren does is he'll put someone in charge of XYZ Company and, as long as that guy is running that satisfactorily, that's good," Halle says. "And he knows he can't run all of these companies. He can't do all of that. He's got some people doing that. And when I look at my position, I think back to somebody like Warren, and I say, 'I'm doing the same thing.' I've got all these people running this organization, and as long as they are all doing their jobs and the results are good, I'm happy. That's what they're supposed to do. Now when that changes, I have to make changes, which is what he does."

Halle relies on his team to pump up sales volumes, control labor costs and increase the total value of each transaction. The balance among the three is sensitive.

Discount Tire sells tires and wheels but doesn't offer oil changes, alignments or general automotive services. By focusing on a limited number of services, the company can reduce customer wait times and build satisfaction. Training expense is reduced, inventory management is simplified, work scheduling is more predictable and units per man-hour can be maximized. By servicing customers faster, the stores can serve more customers per day with the same number of employees and work bays, which leverages the fixed investment in each store.

Increasing the value of each transaction is a more sensitive issue, because each store manager benefits from higher profits but suffers when customers feel pressured or oversold. Employees are trained to explain the various product features to customers and let them make the decision, rather than steering the customer to the most expensive products. The goal is to be the trusted expert for the customer.

"The opposite of a trusted expert in our measurement is a pushy salesman," CFO Christian Roe explains, "and we don't want pushy salesmen driving our customers away."

Employees are encouraged to sell warranty certificates that provide replacement tires in cases not covered by manufacturers' warranties. The certificates are highly profitable to Discount Tire, but they also build customer satisfaction by resolving problems quickly and in the customer's favor.

"For many years in the industry, the only warranties that the tire industry had were workmanship and material failures," Halle remembers. "There were no road hazards. You could get a brand new tire, run over a beer bottle tomorrow and destroy it. Good luck. That's how it was. During that period of time, you would come in and buy a new tire, and next week you'd destroy it. And you'd come into my office, into our store, and I'd feel so bad about that, so what can I do for you? It's a lot of money. It's big money for people, and I'm trying to build a business. So, I start by saying I'm sorry about that, there's no warranty for road hazards like that, but I'll do something for you. And I would do something. I would give you half off or do something, whatever would help the situation. During that period of time—and this is back in Arizona in the early 1970s—I started this warranty program, this certificate program that we have, which has been extremely successful for our company and for all of our customers. People buy that, and then have this failure, and they come in, and here are two new tires. Good-bye and thank you."

The process of tire sales is relatively straightforward, but Discount Tire's approach includes extra steps to instill confidence and loyalty in the customer. The process includes a review of each step of the sale, the product features and costs, what the customer bought and, finally, a thank-you that the team has labeled the "benediction." Making sure to thank the customers and ask them to come back is common sense, at the least, but it's often missed in retail stores.

Sir Tom Farmer, who built the Kwik-Fit chain of automotive stores in Europe and became a friend of Halle's in the 1980s, says Discount Tire's success begins with an understanding of the customer. For the tire buyer, spending hundreds of dollars on new tires is not a joyous shopping experience.

"Nobody gets up in the morning and says, 'What a beautiful day. I think I'll go buy four tires.' They get up and say, 'I have to buy new tires.' It's like going to the dentist," Farmer says.

Because customers tend to view tire buying as a necessary evil, it's not too difficult to exceed their expectations. When Halle started changing snow tires at no charge, the lines extended around the block. Customers responded, as well, when he offered to repair flat tires at no charge and provided free tire inspections. While many financial analysts might consider such freebies unaffordable, Halle found the free services to be highly profitable, especially when the value of referrals is considered.

For the cost of a free tire repair—usually less than $30—Discount Tire can acquire a lifelong customer. While the company might invest $50 to $100 in giving away a tire or two to a cash-strapped driver, that person will come back as a paying customer when he or she is back on firmer financial footing. Along the same lines, Halle never, ever wants his people to lose a customer because a competitor is offering the same tire for a few bucks less.

"We need the customer. The customer doesn't need us," CFO Christian Roe says. "So if you lose a customer over price, you have to buy them back later. It's better to give them the price to get them to stay in the first place."

Discount Tire measures customer satisfaction with a net promoter index, which nets out the difference between customers who would recommend the company and those who would pan it. Only scores of 9 or 10 on a 10-point scale count as positives, and anything below 7 is a negative. Most companies average 5 to 10 percent, according to one study, and a net promoter index over 50 percent is considered solid. Discount Tire consistently scores at the 80 percent level.

When a customer is dissatisfied, the store manager must address the issue personally. At 6:00 p.m. each night, every store manager receives an e-mail with the names of unhappy customers who need to be contacted within twenty-four hours.

Ultimately, the managers will convert many of the unhappy customers into lifelong patrons simply by making a personal connection and offering to solve their problems. This is not rocket science or the stuff of MBA dissertations, but it is highly effective.

"A tire is a commodity," Roe notes. "You can get one elsewhere. The differentiator is the people. By having people with great attitudes, you make the difference for Discount Tire. We hire people with the right personality and the right attitude. We can always teach them how to change tires."

People do business with people they like. Hire, motivate and reward the people that others will like and, no matter what the product, the probability of success rises sharply. It's an impossible way to run a business, but Bruce Halle, like the bumblebee, has found a way to make it fly.

WOODSTOCK FOR TIRE JOCKEYS

Tim Higel pulls up to the opening in the fence that separates the Lakeland Village Resort from the Lakeshore Lodge and Spa on the southern shore of Lake Tahoe. The trip has brought Bruce Halle all of three hundred feet from his rustic cabin on the beach, and Halle might have needed less time to walk the same distance, but Higel won't let the boss walk when he can ride.

Halle is pumped as he alights from the white Chevy Tahoe and strides past the sign that informs of the private party ahead. He stops for a moment to scan the banners that drape the three stories of the Lakeshore Lodge, heralding the fifty years since he rented an old plumbing supply store, built a countertop and started his chain of eight hundred tire stores. Walking past the catering trucks, his pace quickens, and he actually skips the last thirty feet to the registration tables lined with backpacks for the incoming throng.

Halle is the host of this party, but also the guest of honor. The Tahoe trip is the coveted prize for thousands of employees who will compete to move more tires, sell more warranties, shorten wait times and bump up their Customer Delight scores for a chance to spend a few days with Bruce on the California-Nevada border. Each of the twenty-three regions in the Discount Tire Company network is allocated slots for the party, and each regional management team decides which contests to run and how to pass out the rewards.

The corporate office doesn't set the rules for Tahoe, because the corporate office doesn't run the show. Unlike most corporate retreats, it's the workers and not the suits who are the honored guests. And the ticket to entry is earned in the store, where the customers make the ultimate decisions about success.

Some of the "Discount Tire Warriors," as Assistant HR Vice President Staci Adams refers to them, will make the trip three, five or six times as they work their way up from the assistant manager ranks. Halle is always happy to see the familiar faces, of course, but he's most excited for the first-timers. "If you're a guy twenty-three or twenty-four years old, and you're working in a store, and you win a trip like this to Tahoe, it's really cool," he explains, sounding more like one of the twenty-three-year-olds than the captain of industry he's become. To Halle's mind, first-timers should make up the majority of every Tahoe party, even as the most consistent warriors battle for return appearances. "It doesn't do any good to have one guy come there five or six times, and then have people who never get there at all," he argues.

Halle worries about those twenty-three-year-old tire jockeys, and cheers for them to earn the journey to Tahoe. In the Discount Tire network, a trip to Tahoe is a sign of both your recent achievement and your manager's confidence that you're going places in this company.

Halle greets a few of the corporate staffers working the event, then hustles to the cantina set up for afternoon snacks. Anticipating a few hundred carnivores, Men Wielding Fire is offering burritos the size of NBA sneakers, and Halle devours one, observing that his wife wouldn't quite endorse this dining option.

His afternoon repast is interrupted by well-wishers who ask him to pose for cell-phone photos, then shake his hand. Marvin Martinez, a senior assistant manager from Encinitas, California, hustles up to thank him for the $1,000 check Halle sent when Martinez got married the prior year. Halle asks about the wedding and how things are working out for Martinez and his wife.

For the next hour, Halle will burn up all the calories from the burrito as he works his way through the crowd, thanking each person for making the company great and smiling for one more picture.

He moves through a display of old advertisements and photos, mostly from the 1960s, and reappears at the back of the lodge, where the swimming pool is adorned with life-size cutouts of Bruce in various items of beachwear. He doesn't look exactly like Sean Connery in *Dr. No*, but he does appear to be having fun.

As tire store conferees line up for poolside massages, Jason Henderson, an assistant vice president from the Los Angeles region, challenges Halle to take a photo with him under an LA Lakers banner, but the diehard Phoenix Suns fan declines with a laugh.

Halle's son and company president Bruce Jr. shows him the stage the team has set up for evening programs, designed to mimic the first Discount Tire store at 2266 Stadium Boulevard in Ann Arbor, Michigan. Halle notes that the mock-up looks somewhat better than the first store.

The sun is bright and the lake is a glorious blue as hundreds of warriors gather on the beach for the kickoff of Discount Tire's fiftieth anniversary celebration at Tahoe. An airboat zips across the water and makes it only partially up the shore as the Marine Corps Hymn plays and Staff Sergeant Bruce Thomas Halle storms the beachhead. The old Marine clambers up the steps to the stage, pulls a cord to light up the "OPEN" sign on the door, and the party is officially begun.

As he will do dozens or hundreds of times over the next sixty hours, Halle credits the employees for making the company great, for making him proud, and for making each other successful. Gratitude rolls downhill at Discount Tire, with everyone dependent on the success of individual stores, and Halle wants everyone to know the rolling begins with him.

Dinner is early, as the interregional volleyball tournament begins at 6:00 p.m. and most teams are hoping for an upset over perennial winner San Diego. Bob Seger's "Old Time Rock and Roll" blares across the beach as eight regions square off for V-ball glory. Halle stops to watch as San Antonio takes on a team from the corporate office. He doesn't have high hopes for his desk jockeys, but they prove victorious in the end.

By 9:00 p.m., the sun has set behind the mountains as the wind whips the flags of the United States and the states where Discount Tire operates, along with the banners of the company's brands. Swarms of insects flock to the spotlights that illuminate the epic battle between PacWest and New Mexico, while dozens of tire jockeys wait for their turn to talk with Bruce Halle.

Bruce Halle and Bill Sweatt, the former Goodyear executive who is now a consultant and friend to Halle, are chatting under a neon sign for Big Kahuna's beachfront bar. There is no bar—the sign is a remnant of a prior Tahoe celebration—but the staging is apt. One after another, leaders from San Diego, Nevada, Indiana, Ohio and PacWest regions bring their up-and-comers to meet the Big Kahuna.

The conversation is almost always the same. The new guys, and most of the older ones, thank Halle for the opportunity he's given them to work at the company and to come to Tahoe. Halle, in turn, tells them he is the one who is grateful, because the people in the stores are the lifeblood of the business.

Halle and former son-in-law Stuart Wimer, a store manager in Encinitas, California, head to the bar, where a mob from San Antonio appears for thanks and photos. Apart from the dinner break, Halle has been on his feet for more than six hours, and the night is about to get longer as the awards ceremony begins.

CEO Tom Englert, President Bruce Halle Jr., COO Steve Fournier and other corporate execs welcome the partiers and introduce Halle, the giver-in-chief. The crowd chants, "Bruce, Bruce, Bruce," but Halle repeats his mantra: "I'm so proud of you for what you've accomplished. You all came here and you thank me, but you did all the work."

Halle and the executive team fire up the crowd with a mock debate about the number of prizes to be awarded that night. The prize in question is a five-day trip to Hawaii or the Caribbean for the employee and spouse. Even better, days off for a prize trip don't count against vacation time. By the end of the Tahoe trip, Discount Tire will have passed out 153 such awards, with a total value north of half a million dollars.

After the first night's stash of thirty-five prizes has been awarded, Halle and his son work their way down the beach toward the snack tent, but the elder Halle is waylaid as guys from Discount Tire Direct and the Nevada region indoctrinate him in the finer points of beer pong. He watches for fifteen minutes, until the business expert has figured it all out.

"If I was a beer distributor, I'd go broke," he concludes. "Nobody ends up drinking any beer."

Halle plops two slices of pizza on a plate before joining Bill Sweatt, who is rooming with Halle this week. Halle grabs some food for Sweatt and sits for the first time since dinner, roughly five hours ago. It's 11:35 p.m. Halle and Sweatt talk about life for a few minutes before Bruce Jr. sits down and makes plans for a tennis game the next morning. At 11:50, the octogenarian and his friend pick up some oatmeal cookies for the road and call it a night.

Monday and Tuesday at Tahoe bring a steady stream of golf, tennis, bicycle, boat and parasailing excursions, along with massages by the pool. For two hundred guys who work in tire stores all week, the perks are a major motivational tool.

The biggest motivator, though, is Bruce Halle. He's the tire jockey who made it big, who remembers his roots and keeps the doors open for the next generation. One by one, the men in the Discount Tire T-shirts will describe what they see when they look up the corporate ladder, and what they see is themselves. From store managers to assistant regional vice presidents, regional VPs and corporate operations executives, it's a parade of people who started their careers busting tires and, at the top, tire-buster Bruce Halle.

The Tahoe trippers describe Halle as a role model, both for the path of his own life and the path he's opened for them. He's "Mr. Halle," the icon on a pedestal, but they feel comfortable calling him Bruce and, occasionally, slapping him on the back at the bar. The balance is challenging, and most business leaders fail to achieve it. Halle is more a father figure than a boss to many of these people, even though he is clearly the boss.

By Tuesday night, sharp winds from the west are turning the flags into billboards as Houston squares off against San Diego in the volleyball finals. Bruce Halle is standing next to the stands in a pair of shorts and sandals, a white baseball cap and a Discount Tire pullover—one of the items of clothing in the backpacks every attendee received. Employees sitting in the stands offer him a seat, but he declines.

Halle is alone here, both the center of the event and somehow outside of it. It's one of the contradictions in life that the leader of twelve thousand employees is most engaged when talking to one at a time. In a crowd, he appears more comfortable as an observer than as a participant.

He stands five feet from the bleachers, watching San Diego take an early lead with an 18-12 win, smiling as he observes others having fun. Cigar smoke wafts across the beach as Houston ties it up with an 18-8 comeback, and it looks like San Diego, home of beach volleyball, might fall from its throne. In the end, though, San Diego reclaims its crown with an 18-14 win, and it's time for Bruce Halle to hand out some trips.

The awards ceremony is particularly festive as Michael Zuieback, Halle's stepson and executive vice president of corporate strategy, introduces the drivers of Discount Tire's two race cars: drift car racer Daijiro Yoshihara and NASCAR driver Brad Keselowski. Keselowski was NASCAR's top Nationwide Series driver in 2010, despite running out of fuel in one of his races. Zuieback awards him a spare gas can as the crowd roars its approval. The Dallas region team takes a golf trophy, and San Diego receives its volleyball prize, again, but the big question is how many trips the company will give away this night.

Tony Doca, 2009 manager of the year in the Arizona region, is in the crowd, eyeing Assistant Manager Frank Alvarez. Doca has won three trips at Tahoe, but Alvarez, who no longer works with Doca, is here for the first time. Doca decides to follow the Bruce Halle model because "I've been blessed to work for the Bruce Halle family for thirty years and it was time to give back, pay it forward." So when Doca wins his fourth trip, he runs up to the stage and gives his certificate to Alvarez. Alvarez wins a trip a few minutes later and pays it forward to Raul Olivas, who then wins a trip that he hands off to Andy Cazares, "It was really the spirit of Discount Tire," Doca says.

As the drum spins, teammates hug each other and jump up and down as someone from their region wins a trip. Winners race up the front of the stage to claim their prizes, then exit out the back of the stage. For a half hour, the parade of winners continues to fall out the back door of the mock store, staring at their certificates, shaking their heads and, occasionally, weeping.

Sixty-five certificates later, Bruce Halle closes the ceremony, reminding the throng that they are representatives of Discount Tire and that gentlemanly behavior is expected. He made the same comment at the opening ceremony, and the following days included no fights, no furniture thrown into the pool and no notable f-bombs on the beach. Not bad for a party with more than 350 men. And beer.

Bruce Jr., who organized the gathering, thanks his dad and announces one last celebration, a fireworks display that lights up Lake Tahoe and fills the night sky with phosphorous and pride. As the glow fades and the snack tent beckons for the last time, veterans shake their heads and wonder what the company will do next year.

As the rooms empty on Wednesday morning, Bruce Halle and Bill Sweatt are having breakfast together before they depart on separate Discount Tire planes. One after another, the Tahoe trippers come up to shake hands, take photos and offer thanks. As always, Halle turns the tables and credits them for making the company great. As the parade dwindles to a trickle, Halle looks around the tent.

"These guys will all get back home after spending the last few days here and go to work tomorrow," he says, "and the first ten customers to come through the door won't have a chance."

And so ends this year's lesson in employee motivation.

I'M GOING TO BUILD YOU A HOUSE

"Here's what I'm going to do for you," Bruce Halle says, warming up for a story he's told hundreds of times. "I'm going to build you a house. I'm going to pick out a lot, and I'm going to hire an architect, and I'm going to have a house built for you. Then, I'm going to get a decorator in and decorate it all very nicely. And I'm going to give it to you and your wife and, congratulations, it's yours."

He pauses and stares expectantly as his listener considers the possibilities. Halle has a longstanding reputation as a very generous guy, so this could get interesting. Unfortunately, there is a catch.

"All you have to do is pay me for it," he adds. "And, of course, you pay the taxes, and the insurance, and the gas, and electric, the whole thing.

"But it's your house. Enjoy it."

Halle smiles and leans back in his chair as he waits for a response. So far, nobody has agreed to write him the blank check and give up the control that his offer requires. Halle wouldn't take the deal, either. Accepting that much risk and giving up control would be crazy, he says, and crazy is one thing he isn't.

What Halle is, instead, is consistent. Since the day in 1960 when he opened his first store in Ann Arbor, Halle has built more than eight hundred houses for Discount Tire Company.

Of course, the newer stores lack the shag carpeting that gave Store Number One on Stadium Boulevard its special panache, but the fundamentals of the tire business—of retailing in general—haven't changed much in fifty years. And Halle, the octogenarian founder and sole shareholder of Discount Tire Company, isn't a big fan of fixing what ain't broke.

Halle's home-building parable is particularly fitting for a man whose family spent many of his formative years under another family's roof. Halle has little regard for most possessions—he stopped wearing a watch after his older brother, Fred Jr., borrowed and lost the timepiece Bruce had received from their parents. His second wife, Diane, bought him a watch as a wedding gift and he promptly lost it on their honeymoon flight to Hawaii. He has been known to simply leave his car on the street in front of the restaurant where he's dining—with keys in the ignition.

"If I lock the car up, a thief might cut his hand while breaking the window to get in," Halle says, only half joking. "I wouldn't want that on my conscience."

Homes, however, have a different meaning, a meaning that translates to the stores. Each store is home to a Discount Tire family, and the store is where that family will work together to secure the future of each member. Pick the right location for that home, and it will support a large family over a period of decades. Pick the wrong location, and the people inside will suffer.

"I can move the inventory and the equipment from a bad store, but I can't move the store," Halle says simply. "It's not a mistake that's easy to correct."

While Halle has delegated most of the daily tasks of running the company, finding the right place for Discount Tire's next home will always be the chairman's realm. Halle's site selection performance has been well above average. Of thirty-six stores open at the end of 1979, thirty-five remained in operation in 2011—more than three decades later.

This longevity results in large part from the talent and commitment of the people who live in the stores each day. Before the employees get there, however, Bruce Halle walks the property, considering its potential.

"We haven't made many real estate mistakes, because we get personally involved in the process," says General Counsel James Silhasek. "You can get all kinds of data and pictures of a parcel, but that isn't enough. You have to make a personal visit, see the traffic flow, measure the curb appeal of the property and so on. We recently saw a property in Seattle; it looked great on paper, but a personal visit showed that you needed to take a bridge that doesn't exist to get to the closest major road."

If Halle needed any reinforcement of his commitment to boots on the ground, that endorsement came from longtime friend Karl Eller, onetime chair of Circle K and, later, Clear Channel Outdoor. In building Circle K to more than five thousand convenience/gas stores in the 1980s, Eller allowed his team to sign up for sites on the recommendation of real estate representatives, often without walking the property himself.

"We wanted to build our penetration of stores in California, so I told my real estate people they would get a bonus for finding good stores. I think there were twelve or thirteen of them, and I tried to look at all of them but I didn't get to it," Eller recalls. The company ended up with unprofitable or marginally profitable sites with poor visibility, limited signage opportunities and limited ingress and egress.

It's a mistake Eller wouldn't make again, and neither would Halle. In 2011, Halle and Silhasek journeyed with other members of senior management to visit 204 potential store locations across Discount Tire's twenty-three regions. Regional vice presidents work with local real estate agents to identify the sites they'll recommend, but no discussions of details are permitted until after the boss has walked the property.

On this particular day, the property under consideration is in Florida, a market the company entered in 1989 and struggled to bring to profitability. Well-entrenched competitors limited Discount Tire's progress for several years, and the company considered cutting its losses and pulling back from the market. Halle refused to give in, arguing that showing weakness in Florida would embolden competitors to move into his stronger markets. Finally, more than a decade later, the ink flowed from red to black.

"If we let them win on their turf," Halle says now, "that would encourage them to come after us on our turf. And that would have been more expensive than fighting it out in Florida. If I'm going to have a war, I want it in their backyard, not mine."

Greg Smith, regional vice president for Florida, and Assistant Vice President Gary Dunlap are waiting at Pensacola Aviation Center as the fourteen-passenger Falcon—one of three Discount Tire jets—taxis to the terminal. Smith and Dunlap are looking to add at least two more stores in this area, hoping to gain some economies of scale. They ferry the corporate team to the first site, an outlot in a shopping center anchored by a Home Depot. As seven sets of dress shoes alight on the cracked asphalt— Halle insists that all executives wear suits to work—the wisdom of walking the site becomes apparent.

Overall, the general location is attractive. Home Depot customers tend to fit the demographic of Discount Tire customers, and there's another demographic match, a McDonald's restaurant, about a quarter mile to the south. There are no other stores in the eastern roadside outlots of this shopping center, though, and the large building across the eight-lane road, once a furniture store, sits empty.

Gary Van Brunt, who joined Halle at his first store in 1962 and serves as vice chairman today, looks down the road toward the McDonald's. "Is anything available over there?" he asks. As it turns out, another lot is on the market at a higher asking price. Seven executives pile back into the cars and drive several hundred feet to the south. The second outlot is closer to the McDonald's restaurant and closer to the corner of North Davis Highway and Brent. Expressway ramps are just west on Brent, and the alternate location offers higher visibility to more traffic. Roughly one thousand feet could make the difference between yes and no.

The team discusses the seller's asking price, but any detailed discussions will wait until Smith has shown all the sites and the management team is back in the air. After they leave Florida the next day, they'll judge the asking price as too high in relation to overall real estate market trends and hold back on making any offers.

Scouting sites never gets old, Halle says, and there is no point of diminishing returns in his mind as the number of existing stores climbs. Halle is a retail thinker. Each person is unique, each customer is unique and each store is unique—and all are of equal merit in his worldview.

"The first store went okay, then the second store was pretty good as well," he says. "The five-hundredth store was a milestone, but it's no more or less important than any other store."

Having built hundreds of stores, Halle has learned that there's much more to real estate than the oft-cited location, location and location. Buying an existing tire store, he says, is seldom the most inspired choice.

"When you get somebody else's store, you are getting their reputation too," he warns. "You repaint the building and put a different sign on it, but a customer is driving down the street and sees that tire store and thinks, *I had a hell of a bad experience there. I'll never go there again.* He doesn't even know it's changed its name or ownership, so that hurts. When we pick up somebody else's store, it takes three times longer to make it profitable."

The company will buy those problems when necessary, partly because tire stores aren't the most sought-after tenants for most shopping center owners. The revenues are low, space needs are high and there's no fashionable mystique to one more set of automotive bays facing the parking lot. Often, the best space available in a market is already filled by another tire store.

In the 1980s, Discount Tire bought twenty-five Goodyear tire stores to accelerate its expansion into southern California. The sites represented strong potential, but they also suffered from bad memories among former Goodyear customers. Discount Tire's signage looks nothing like Goodyear's, but customers would often look at the building simply as the store they didn't like. True to Halle's expectation, the process of building reputation and profitability was slower than is the case for newly built properties.

Nearly twenty years later, the challenge continues, this time in the context of lease renewals. Shopping center owners want a share of store profits as a component of lease payments, and paying the landlord leaves less money to pay employees—or Halle.

"That's one of the disadvantages of leases that we assumed from other people with not much time left," according to Halle. "It's actually been twenty years since we did this, but time runs out; twenty years go fast."

Discount Tire will lease locations when absolutely essential, but the clear preference is to own, not rent. The company owns approximately 80 percent of the properties that house its stores, and with stores that remain in business twenty, thirty or more years, the long-term benefits are clear.

Beyond the financial considerations for the individual stores, Halle is determined to build only in areas where his employees—including part-time tire techs—can afford to live. Halle watched with dismay as the cost of living rose sharply after he started building stores in Santa Fe, New Mexico, leading him to raise salaries 25 percent to help his employees keep up.

Recent expansion has focused on regions like Georgia and Tennessee, where facilities and operating costs are affordable and employees can raise families on the income they earn at Discount Tire. While high-cost regions like the mid-Atlantic states can limit store margins, the economics for employees are even worse, according to Halle.

"The problem is that the cost of living for our people is terrible. It's awful," Halle explains. "You can't afford to buy a house. Once you get into the northern part of Virginia, approaching the DC, Maryland area, the cost of living is astronomical, so our guys can't buy a home there. The cost of living is terrible, and you don't collect any more for your merchandise."

Even with his focus on affordable communities, it's a major challenge to build new homes as quickly as Halle's managers can fill them. With around eight hundred stores in operation, Discount Tire has the bench strength to open eighty to a hundred stores or more each year. But the company's strategic plan includes a mandate to "grow responsibly," and the capital requirements are daunting. At roughly $3 million to build, open, equip and stock a company-owned store, one hundred stores would require an annual investment of $300 million, which is outside Halle's comfort level for debt and risk.

Instead, the company is targeting forty to fifty new stores per year, which translates into a $120 million annual fixed investment if the stores are all owned rather than leased, a 5 percent growth rate for stores and a long queue for potential store managers. The management team has learned the lessons of companies that, like armies, moved too far ahead of their supply lines. Halle and his team won't grow as fast as possible, because they are unwilling to spread capital or manpower across too broad a network. As Halle sees it, employees are better off being well compensated in a stable company than they would be in a risky environment of overly rapid growth.

Even with a "responsible growth" strategy in place, the target of forty to fifty new stores has Halle walking several times that many sites each year. Once a site is chosen, it can take a year or more to build and open a store, and most of the long-term benefits from those stores will accrue to a company that no longer includes Bruce Halle. While Halle's father lived to be ninety-two, and the chairman continues to enjoy robust health, most octogenarians would not be placing bets with a thirty-year payoff.

Halle is aware that his time with the company will come to a close someday, but that's a decision for The Boss to make. As long as The Boss allows him the opportunity, Halle will keep building the company as if he will always be there to lead it. His wife, Diane, has led him into a more aggressive estate planning process, forcing him to prepare for the needs of both the company and his own family in case he does not live forever. The plan is largely complete, Halle says, with a mechanism to keep the company private, out of the clutches of Wall Streeters and their ilk.

Within the company, most of the management team is confident that the culture and systems are sustainable, that Discount Tire has the people and drive to continue to thrive without its founder.

In one sense, Halle is irreplaceable. Someone else can be the chairman, but nobody else can fill his shoes as founder. The question "What would Bruce do?" does not transfer to anyone else in the organization.

At the same time, the twenty-three regions and more than eight hundred stores are filled with lost boys who swallowed the pill and agreed to follow Halle, as Al Olsen said forty-five years earlier, "'til death do us part." Maintaining the culture and creating the opportunity for the next generation of Discount Tire families is not the job of Bruce Halle anymore, according to many of his executives. Now, it's the job of everyone in the company.

"His philosophy is to treat people like you want to be treated," says Bruce Halle Jr. of his dad. "He's a fair, honest, generous guy. That's been spread down. That's how everyone else is expected to be. Now, that philosophy is passed down through the vice presidents in the regions and it goes all the way down. That's the hard part about a business, just keeping that culture."

With the culture well established and a strong team behind him, Halle could take much more time off as a non-executive chairman and watch as his people sustain his creation. Most people would give some thought to the pace of his travel schedule and the incremental value of one more store in a company with eight hundred similar outposts. Most people would let somebody else trek across the vacant lots in search of a new store that might not be built within his lifetime.

Bruce Thomas Halle isn't most people, though, and, today, he's made a promise to build someone a house.

ABOUT THE AUTHOR

Michael Rosenbaum is a business consultant and former financial journalist who has both studied and advised hundreds of corporate leaders over his career.

As president of the nation's largest investor relations agency, Rosenbaum managed operations of a $35 million business with five offices and three hundred employees. At that agency, he advised CEOs and CFOs at more than 150 companies regarding strategic financial and marketing issues. He holds both a bachelor's degree in communications and a master's degree in business administration and is an active member of the World Presidents' Organization.

Other books by Michael Rosenbaum include

- *[Your Name Here] Guide to Life: The Book You'd Have Written, If Only You Had the Time*
- *Building Value Through Investor Relations*
- *The Governance Game* (coauthored with Marilyn Seymann)
- *Selling Your Story to Wall Street: The Art & Science of Investor Relations*